The Kurdish Women of Turkey:
Building a Nation, Struggling for Gender Parity

The Moshe Dayan Center for Middle Eastern and African Studies seeks to contribute by research, documentation, and publication to the study and understanding of the modern history and current affairs of the Middle East and Africa. The Center is part of the School of History and the Lester and Sally Entin Faculty of Humanities at Tel Aviv University.

The Kurdish Women of Turkey: Building a Nation, Struggling for Gender Parity

Heidi Basch-Harod

TEL AVIV UNIVERSITY

MDC

The Moshe Dayan Center for
Middle Eastern and African Studies

Table of Contents

Dedicated to Serafina Galletti, Maria Angela Basch,
Maayan Shoshana Harod, and Meital Devorah Harod

Acknowledgements

In hindsight, the seed of this monograph was planted in March of 2004 when Margery Farrar, Human Rights Specialist to U.S. Representative Tom Lantos, handed me Leyla Zana's *Writings from Prison*. It was then that I first became acquainted with the Kurdish aspiration for self-determination and one of many extraordinary women in this ongoing struggle. Najat Hirbawi, of the Palestine-Israel *Journal* in East Jerusalem, opened my eyes to the every day acts of resistance – both present and historic, personal and national – that women in the region carry out in an attempt to maintain dignity in undignified situations. Prof. Ofra Bengio, for encouraging and pushing me to be precise, thorough, fair, and for fueling my determination to tell a story I hope will be a source of interest and inspiration to many. Prof. Bruce Maddy-Weitzman, for always making time for brainstorming, ruminating, and mentoring. Prof. Uzi Rabi, for giving me a place to call home in Israel, and a space to make a difference. I am eternally grateful to these professors for bestowing their unique knowledge, wisdom, and expertise. And to all those who spend most of their waking hours on the 4th floor of the Gilman Building where the Moshe Dayan Center for Middle Eastern and African Studies resides, your energy, passion, and camaraderie continue to make this work a privilege and pleasure; it is an honor to be your colleague. Elena Kuznetsov-Lesnick, for her skills and patience. Martin and Maria Basch, for your dedication to thewellbeing and success of your three children. Eitan Harod, for encouraging me, and insisting I finish what I start.

List of Initials and Acronyms

AKP – Adalet ve Kalkınma Partisi, Justice and Development Party
BDP – Baris ve Demokrasi Partisi, Peace and Democracy Party
CHP – Cumhuriyet Halk Partisi, Republican People's Party
DEP – Demokrasi Partisi, Democracy Party
DEHAP – Demokratik Halk Partisi, Democratic People's Party
DTP – Demokratik Toplum Partisi, Democratic Society Party
DÖKH – Demokratik Özgür Kadın Hareketi, Democratic and Free Women Movement
HEP – Halkın Emek Partisi, People's Labor Party
HDP – Halkların Demokratik Partisi, The People's Democratic Party
İHD – İnsan Hakları Derneği, Human Rights Association
KA-MER – Kadın Merkezi, Women's Center Foundation
KCK – Koma Civakên Kurdistan, Kurdish Communities Union
KHRP – Kurdish Human Rights Project
KJB – Koma Jinên Bilind, High Women's Council
KRG – Kurdistan Regional Government
PAJK – Partiya Azadiya Jin a Kurdistan, Kurdistan Women's Liberation Party
PJKK – Partiya Jinên Karkerên Kurdistanê, Kurdistan Working Women's Party
PKK – Partiya Karkerên Kurdistan, Kurdistan Workers' Party
SHP – Sosyal Demokrat Halkçi Parti, Social Democrat Populist Party
TBMM – Türkiye Büyük Millet Meclisi, The Grand National Assembly of Turkey
YJA – Yektiyên Jinên Azad, Free Women's Union
YJA-Star – Yektiyên Jinên Azad Star, Free Women's Union-Star
YAJK – Yekîtiya Azadiya Jinên Kurdistanê, Kurdistan Free Women's Union
YJWK – Yêkitîya Jinên Welatparêzên Kurdistanê, the Union of the Patriotic Women of Kurdistan

Introduction

The Kurds, a stateless people constituting approximately 30 million inhabitants of the Middle East, constitute one of the largest populations in the region.[1] Living a simultaneously shared and separate destiny written in the aftermath of World War I, today the majority of Kurds reside in the adjacent areas of Iran, Iraq, Syria, and Turkey. Separated by borders and circumstances, the four parts of Kurdistan: Rojhalat (east, Iran), Bashur (south, Iraq), Bakur (north, Turkey), and Rojava (west, Syria) remain detached. With the hope of building cohesion among a people historically challenged by internal diversity and external adversaries, early-twentieth century Kurdish nationalist movements propagated an imagined community[2] to prevent the disenfranchisement that indeed befell the Kurds in the years following World War I. In the twenty-first century, the geopolitical situation of the Kurds continues to render them a fragmented nation. As recent history has unfolded, fueled by linguistic differences, opposing tribal loyalties, and state policies created with the purpose of ensuring dislocation of the Kurds, one from the other, Kurdish nation-building is marked by disparateness, disconnect, and rivalry.

This complicated past, however, has not stopped the Kurds in their quest for self-determination. While there is little measurable progress toward cohesion among Kurds in their national aspirations, in the late-twentieth century and into the twenty-first century, a new element in the Kurdish story developed: the role, function, and significance of Kurdish women in the ongoing ethno-national movement. Although largely overlooked, it is increasingly difficult to ignore the contributions of Kurdish women to these efforts and developments. But just as the Kurds and their national movements are fragmented, women's involvement in Kurdish nation-building has been divided as well. Thus, the time frame of this book begins with the rise of Turkish nationalism in the decades leading up to World War I, and focuses solely on the Kurds of Turkey and the role of Kurdish women in the Kurdish nation-building movement there.

Starting in the late nineteenth century, the "Turkification" of the Ottoman Empire propelled the proponents of Kurdish nationalism to formulate a competing national narrative that distinguished the Kurds, in particular, from

---

1. Ofra Bengio (ed.), *Kurdish Awakening: Nation Building in a Fragmented Homeland*, (Austin, TX: University of Texas Press, 2014).
2. Sherko Kirmanj, "Kurdish Integration in Iraq: the Paradoxes of Nation Formation and Nation Building," in Ofra Bengio (ed.), *Kurdish Awakening: Nation Building in a Fragmented Homeland*, (Austin, TX: University of Texas Press, 2014), pp. 91–95.

their Turkish and Arab-Ottoman counterparts. Fearful of popular discourse that denied the Kurds recognition as a separate nation from the Turks, Kurdish nationalists sought to gain Western support. In 1913, a Kurdish writer informed the readers of his publication, *Kurdish Press*, that the entire West and parts of the East were preoccupied with the "woman question."[3] The "woman question" informed the discussion of the changing political, economic, and professional roles of women that included suffrage movements in the United States and Great Britain, in addition to social and sexual liberation activities.[4] Kurdish intellectuals leading the Kurdish nationalist movement saw in the "woman question" a tactic with which to attract Western support for their cause.

An arguably falsified image of Kurdish women, endowed with agency in comparison to other Ottoman female populations, was thus disseminated in literature and discussion so as to present the Kurds as supporters of modernity, known to be valued by Western powers.[5] Subsequently the "woman question" and cause became a vehicle to differentiate Kurdish identity from Turkish, Persian, Arab, and other Ottoman peoples, and to advocate for the legitimacy of Kurdish nationalism. In reality, however, very few women were engaged in this movement that claimed Kurdish women as viable and valuable members of the Kurdish socio-political fabric.

World War I ended with the demise of the Ottoman Empire and led to the establishment of the Republic of Turkey. In the Empire's wake, the rise of a strong and exclusively Turkish state led to persecution of the Kurdish national cause and the targeted denial of Kurdishness — including bans on Kurdish language and culture, internal displacement, and exile. During this period of time, known as the silent decades, both the Kurdish national cause and the Kurdish "woman question" were put on hold. It was not until the mid to late 1960s that Kurdish women were once again viewed as utile toward the realization of Kurdish nationalist ambitions. Unlike the early twentieth century Kurdish national movement, however, Kurdish women in the present ethno-national struggle have taken the narrative into their own hands — both as Kurds and as women. They are dissatisfied with their existence under a hegemonic Turkish state, as well as with the struggles they face as members of a fiercely patriarchal Kurdish society.

---

3. Janet Klein, "En-Gendering Nationalism," in Shahrzad Mojab (ed.), *Women of a Non-State Nation: The Kurds* (Costa Mesa, CA: Mazda Publishers, 2001), p. 25.
4. Janine Utell, "The Woman Question," The Modernist Journals Project, a joint project of Brown University and University of Tulsa, accessed March 14, 2015.
5. Klein, "En-Gendering Nationalism," pp. 28–29.

The Omission of Kurdish Women's Role
in Nation-Building

According to Shahrzad Mojab, a leading scholar and prolific author on the topic of Kurdish women, while the Kurds are the fourth largest nation in the Middle East, discourse on women in the region largely overlooks Kurdish women.[6] Their omission, Mojab argues, is due to the fact that they represent a stateless demographic in the Middle East and therefore lack coherent political recourse. Despite her claim that it is the statelessness of Kurdish women that excludes them from discussion as well as hinders their progress, particularly since the late 1990s, one of the most influential factors enabling Kurdish women to advance in their struggle for gender parity is the fact that it is being carried out in the context of, and often against, the Turkish state.

In fact, it is the experience of the state that shapes and defines the dimensions of this movement. In order to illustrate this, a number of threads of political and civil engagement, both within Turkey and outside its borders, must be intertwined. Namely, the establishment and evolution of the PKK (Kurdistan Workers' Party) and its early inclusion of women; the internal political climate and domestic policy in Turkey towards the Kurds, in part influenced by Turkey's hopes for accession to EU membership (a process that has also positively affected Turkey's gender policy reform); the increasing civil and political engagement of Kurdish women, on-the-ground, in Turkey; the support of women in the Kurdish Diaspora (particularly in Europe), as well as general international support for the cause of Kurdish women; and the manifestations of all of these factors, which materialize within the context of the modern nation-state of the Republic of Turkey and its response to these variables.

Feminist scholar, Valentine M. Moghadam, claims that, historically, movements in the region "for national liberation and revolutionary states have not always extended principles of autonomy and liberation to women."[7] Instead, quite often in national struggles, women's behavior, appearance, and the "acceptable range of their activities" become subject to the "political or

---

6. Shahrzad Mojab and Rachel Gorman, "Dispersed Nationalism: War, Diaspora and Kurdish Women's Organizing," *Journal of Middle East Women's Studies*, Vol. 3, No. 1 (Winter 2007), pp. 58–85; Nira Yuval-Davis, *Gender and Nation* (London: Sage Publications, 1997), pp. 46–47, 58; Valentine M. Moghadam, *Gender and Nationality: Women and Politics in Muslim Societies* (London and New Jersey: Zed Books Ltd., 1994), p. 150. Kurdish women are primarily, scattered in the four adjacent regions of Iraq, Iran, Syria and Turkey.

7. Valentine M. Moghadam, *Gender and National Identity: Women and Politics in Muslim Societies* (London and New Jersey: Zed Books Ltd., 1994).

cultural objectives of political movements, states, and leaderships."[8] In the case of Kurdish women in Turkey, however, autonomy was extended to, and has also been claimed by women active in the ethno-national struggle. Uniquely, the growing national movement could not, did not, and does not stymie the evolution of Kurdish women's agency.

The developments in the Kurdish women's movement in Turkey challenge Mojab and Moghadam's otherwise accurate observation that, although nationalist movements, inherently gendered in the twentieth and twenty-first century Middle East,[9] depend on the support of both men and women, they discourage any manifestation of womanhood or political demands for gender equality.[10] (In many other examples of women's movements that arise from a nationalist struggle, such as those of Iran, Algeria, and the Palestinians, this claim continues to hold true.) Unprecedentedly, a concomitant outcome of the Kurdish ethno-national movement in Turkey is the equally persistent campaign — led by Kurdish women and supported by increasing numbers of Kurdish men — to promote women's rights and to create a society that does not view half of its population as inferior.

The Paradoxical State of Kurdish Women in Turkey

As of 2009, statistics gathered in Turkey indicate that nearly 42 percent of all Turkish and Kurdish women older than 15, and 47 percent of women living in rural areas (a majority of whom are Kurds) experienced physical or sexual violence at the hands of a husband or partner at some point in their lives.[11] More than 70 percent of Kurdish women have not completed primary school, and less than 0.5 percent have completed secondary education.[12] According to data collected in 2011 by KONDA, a public opinion research and consultancy agency in Turkey, 38 percent of women in Turkey's Kurdish regions are illiterate, while

---

8. Hanna Papanek, "The Ideal Woman and the Ideal Society: Control and Autonomy in the Construction of Identity," in V. M. Moghadam (ed.), *Identity Politics and Women*, (Boulder, CO: Westview Press, 1994).

9. Moghadam, *Gender and Nationality: Women and Politics in Muslim Societies*, p. 1.

10. Shahrzad Mojab, "Nationalism and Feminism: The Case of Kurdistan," in *Institute Simone de Beauvoir Bulletin* (Montreal: Concordial University Press, 1995), p. 65–73.

11. Human Rights Watch, "He Loves You, He Beats You: Family Violence in Turkey and Access to Protection," *Human Rights Watch*, May 4, 2011, p. 5, accessed May 26, 2011.

12. Metin Yüksel, "The Encounter of Kurdish Women with Nationalism in Turkey," *Middle Eastern Studies*, Vol. 42, No. 5 (Sept. 2006), p. 779.

in other areas of the country percentages range from zero to eight.[13] Unlike Kurdish men, who learn Turkish during their compulsory army service, Kurdish women in rural areas as well as in urban Kurdish enclaves often do not speak Turkish, the sole official language of Turkey. These persistent trends, among many other difficulties arising from their situation, continue to prevent women from accessing social services, receiving an education, and pursuing employment.[14] Consequently, most Kurdish women in Turkey continue to suffer from illiteracy and political disenfranchisement. Their ethnic identity as Kurds also makes them targets of state violence in the ongoing struggle between the Kurds and the Turkish ethnocentric state. Quite often, the plight of Kurdish women is aptly described as one of "double oppression."

Yet, over the past three decades, and especially since the 1990s, tens of thousands of Kurdish women in Turkey have played and continue to play an increasingly active and visible role in the Kurdish national movement currently taking place in Turkey. As an outgrowth of their involvement, a distinct movement campaigning for Kurdish women's rights has also arisen and is enjoying incremental measures of success across the socio-political and economic spectra.

Paradoxically, despite disheartening statistics describing Kurdish women's lives, Kurdish women in today's Turkey are parliamentarians, political organizers, social activists, lawyers, guerilla fighters, poets, artists, and academics. Increasing numbers of young Kurdish women have access to basic education and seek employment outside of the home with the blessing of their families.[15] With respect to Kurdish history, these developments mark a striking break from the past. With respect to women's history in the Middle East, the strides of Kurdish women in Turkey is, thus far, unmatched.

---

13. Eva Bernard, "Women and the Kurdish Movement in Turkey: "There will be no turning back," *The WVoice*, Vol. 2, No. 4, May 8, 2014, accessed May 24, 2014.

14. Eda S, "We Can Change…" Finalist in WLPS Youth Essay Contest Group 2: 18–25 years, January 16, 2011, accessed April 25, 2011.

15. Anonymous, Personal Interview, March 20, 2011.

Chapter 1

The Social Code and Conduct of the Typical Kurdish Woman in Turkey

Most historic images of Kurdish women come from sources written in English, French, German, and Italian. These chronicles date as far back as the seventeenth century and come from those passing through the region, including diplomats, Catholic missionaries, and merchants; and, in the late eighteenth century, military officers, civil servants, archaeologists, botanists, Protestant missionaries, and female travelers.[16] From this literature, contemporary scholars of Kurdish women's history agree that Westerners exhibited the tendency to depict "Kurdish women as enjoying more freedom than Turkish, Persian, and Arab women," based on observations that Kurdish women did not wear the veil and associated with men in public.[17] Scholars also attribute this consensus to the handful of influential women that appear in writings on Kurdish history (discussed in Chapter Two).

These conclusions, however, contributed to a misunderstanding of Kurdish women's socio-cultural standing, and led to a canon of misinformation on the topic, manipulated by various stakeholders at different points in time. For example, with the rise of Turkish nationalism in the pre-World War I era, Kurdish intellectuals began to decry policies they viewed as "Turkifying Kurds."[18] In their efforts to differentiate Kurds from Turks, Janet Klein's research shows that proponents of Kurdish nationalism emphasized "the distinctness of Kurdish women," vis-à-vis their Turkish, Arab, and other Muslim-Ottoman

---

16. Mirella Galletti, "Western Images of Women's Role in Kurdish Society," in Shahrzad Mojab (ed.), *Women of a Non-State Nation: The Kurds* (Costa Mesa, CA: Mazda Publishers, 2001), p. 209.

17. Mojab, "Nationalism and Feminism: The Case of Kurdistan," p. 65; Mirella Galletti, "Western Images of Women's Role in Kurdish Society," p. 209; H.H. Hansen, *The Kurdish Woman's Life: Field Research in Muslim Society*, Iraq (Copenhagen: Nationalmuseets Skrifter, Etnografisk, Roekke VII, 1961), p. 7.

18. Janet Klein, "En-Gendering Nationalism: The 'Woman Question' in Kurdish Nationalist Discourse of the Late Ottoman Period," in Shahrzad Mojab (ed.), *Women of a Non-State Nation: The Kurds* (Costa Mesa, CA: Mazda Publishers, Inc., 2001).

counterparts in order to denounce and reject arguments that denied the Kurds recognition as a separate nation.[19] Kurdish nationalists found that propagation of a typical Kurdish woman's image as a free agent, who "is the head of the household...[and who] has blended into the social life in which men, too, find themselves, occupying a respectable station,"[20] appealed to Western support and sensitivities surrounding the self-determination discourse and its inclusion of the status of women, two issues that characterized the political zeitgeist of the early twentieth century. These representations, though, were selective, served a particular political agenda, and ignored the hardships and restrictions Kurdish women endured precisely because of their gender. The reality of Kurdish women was and is much more nuanced.

Nevertheless, until the mid-twentieth century, the writings of history largely omitted discussion and analysis of Kurdish women's existence in a society formed around patriarchal structures. Within these sociological edifices, factors such as family and tribal affiliation determined an individual's status and relations. This created a social framework that kept Kurdish women in a "subordinate position within [a] feudal social system."[21]

Yet, despite the shortcomings of individual sources, the compiled works of Kurdish history offer a multi-layered understanding of Kurdish women's status over time. Also, the variegated observations of different classes of Kurdish women and the diverse environments in which they lived provide insight into how the past continues to inform Kurdish women's present-day roles and challenges. The resulting paradox — in which Kurdish women strive to break with a pre-determined past in an environment of new possibilities — inspires greater appreciation for the changes catalyzed by the Kurdish women of Turkey in the late twentieth and early twenty-first centuries.

Representations of Kurdish Women in History

According to the chronicles of Carsten Niebuhr, a German traveler who visited the Kurdish territories of today's Turkey in the eighteenth century, the Kurds differed from the Arabs in that they evinced greater pleasure at the

---

19. Klein, "En-Gendering Nationalism," p. 37.
20. Ibid.
21. International Free Women's Foundation (Rotterdam, Utrecht University, Department of Clinical and Health Psychology) and Kurdistan Information Office, Paris, conducted and edited, *Psychological Consequences of Trauma Experiences on the Development of Migrated Kurdish Women in the European Union: Final Results and Background of a Survey in Five European Countries and Turkey* (Rotterdam: International Free Women's Foundation, 2007), p. 39.

birth of a daughter than a son, "as a good bride price could be obtained for her, accompanied by only a small trousseau."[22] Mirella Galletti identifies the Dominican priest, Giuseppe Campanile, who lived in the area of Kurdistan between 1802 and 1815 as the author of the first complete book focusing on Kurdistan, which also included a description of its female inhabitants. In his observations, Campanile remarked on the smoking habits and caffeine consumption of Kurdish women (married and unmarried), their proclivity for superstition, and modes of dress and jewelry.[23] He also recorded the domestic habits of Kurdish women vis-à-vis their husband and children. For example, he saw that Kurdish women served their husbands meals, but never ate with them, and that women took the leavings their husbands did not consume. He described the Kurdish women he saw as their husbands' slaves, "as they carry food, cools [sic], pipe, coffee…and everything he needs."[24] In contrast, he also made note of women in Mosul (in today's Iraq), who sold pearls in the public marketplace; as well as those who participated in the women's-only picnic — a *serin* — that wealthy and common women held twice a year, where men were not allowed and they could "sing, dance, and eat until nightfall when they returned home."[25]

In 1859, the Kurdish writer Mela (Mullah) Mahmud Bayazidi wrote a book called, *Customs and Manners of the Kurds*, in which he outlined the social conditions of Kurdish women in the mid-nineteenth century. Matching other travelers' observations of these women, he noted that Kurdish women could be seen working, dancing, and singing together with men and were visible outside, unveiled.[26] Although Mela Mahmud argued "tribal and rural Kurdish women were as free as the women of Europe" because they publicly socialized with men, he also noted that Kurdish women who engaged in pre-marital or extra-marital relationships with a "stranger" would be "killed without hesitation and with impunity." (According to traditional Kurdish social customs, only murder can restore the shamed family, its village and, by extension, its tribe's compromised honor.) Moreover, he claimed, these periodic honor killings instilled fear in a woman so that her priority would be the protection of her modesty and chastity, and the knowledge that if her family failed to carry out her execution, they too would be outcasts in their society.[27]

---

22. Hansen, *The Kurdish Woman's Life*, p. 123.
23. Galletti, "Western Images of Women's Role in Kurdish Society," p. 210.
24. Ibid., p. 211.
25. Ibid.
26. International Free Women's Foundation, Psychological Consequences, p. 24.
27. Shahrzad Mojab and Amir Hassanpour, "In Memory of Fadime Sahindal, Thoughts on the Struggle Against 'Honor Killing'," *KWAHK*, October 17, 2002, accessed December 12, 2011.

In 1908, British Colonel Mark Sykes submitted an extensive report on the Kurdish tribes of the Ottoman Empire to the Royal Anthropological Institute of Great Britain and Ireland. The report included findings from 7,500 miles of "riding and innumerable conversations with policemen, muleteers, mullahs, chieftains, sheep drovers, horse dealers, carriers and other people capable of giving one first hand [sic] information."[28] Although women were not a main feature of his reports, Sykes did include his observations and conclusions about Kurdish women that provided for another eyewitness account of the diverse range of roles and appearances of Kurdish women, which differed from clan to clan and tribe to tribe.

Among the semi-nomadic Kurds of the Iraqi Kurdistan region and Iran, which he classified as "Baban Kurds," Sykes commented on the strikingly beautiful women of this group, who were "allowed great freedom," and who rode and shot as well as men, "but who undertake no manual labour beyond making butter and performing ordinary household duties."[29] Of the Kurdish "sedentary mountaineers" of the Ottoman Empire, he remarked, "Like the Baban Kurds their women do not veil and are well treated."[30] Around the area of Dersim (today's Tunceli in Turkey), Sykes describes tribes "who live in a kind of feudal vassalage to Beys [sic] who talk Turkish and veil their women," and who he claims were "apparently Pagans, who call themselves Shias."[31]

Other tribes clearly were not pleasing to Sykes' aesthetic taste. This becomes apparent in his identification of "Class III" Kurds, semi-nomadic mountaineers who were "of a thievish disposition, bloodthirsty, cowardly and often cruel. Their women are ugly and hard worked, they usually ride with donkeys or mules, and are extremely erratic in their movements."[32] Conversely, among the D'sdie clan he noted that their women were "exceedingly handsome and affect a peculiar and distinctive dress, i.e., blue turbans like the men, and dark heavy garments, no colour or ornaments of any kind being worn."[33] In his comments on the women of the nomadic Herki tribe, found near Van and Erzurum, he remarked that women were "very bold and manly."[34]

---

28. Mark Sykes, "The Kurdish Tribes of the Ottoman Empire," *The Journal of the Royal Anthropological Institute of Great Britain and Ireland*, Vol. 38 (Jul.-Dec. 1908), pp. 451–486.
29. Sykes, "The Kurdish Tribes of the Ottoman Empire," p. 454.
30. Ibid.
31. Ibid., p. 467.
32. Ibid., p. 455.
33. Ibid..
34. Ibid., p. 458.

In other areas of the Ottoman Empire he observed that Kurdish women, while dressing in a fashion similar to the Turkish-speaking people of Anatolia, wore the veil in front of Muslims and Christians.[35] In contrast, among the Jibranli tribe, purportedly living most of the year near Diyarbakır, the "Jibranli women shave the top of their heads as do the men."[36]

In the travel notes of British Political Officer C.J. Edmonds, who roamed the area of Northeastern Iraq from 1919 to 1925, he wrote that among the "nomadic tribes between the plains of Iraq and the highlands of Persia and Turkey…jolly young women sometimes carrying a rifle, [and] babies with their faces poking out of saddle bags" were a common sight.[37] In a rare, more nuanced observation, he continued: "In the villages Kurdish women probably have as bad a time as any of their neighbors in the Middle East, being saddled with much of the drudgery; among the most unpleasant of tasks and carrying on their backs leaky skins of icy water from village spring to house — something a man is never seen doing."[38]

Further observations by Edmonds, enumerated below, offer a look into the socio-cultural and economic practices of common Kurdish women that happen to concur with older as well as more recent studies of the same populations. Again, the links between history and the present day demonstrate a continuous practice of certain customs that still affect the lives of Kurdish women and shape Kurdish society's social code, which ultimately governs the actions and life choices of its women. In the study of the Kurdish women of Turkey, it is important to bear in mind this continuum of tradition, as it highlights the complicated space between the past and the present that Kurdish women continue to inhabit.

The Burden of *Namus*

Traditionally, conservative, male-dominated Kurdish society determines the life trajectory of its women. In this social framework, women are not perceived as individuals, but rather essential components instrumental in upholding a strict code of social conduct. According to this system, Iranian Kurdish linguistic scholar, Amir Hassanpour, claims that females in Kurdish society, married or not, are accepted as members of the family, tribe, community, and nation on

---

35. Sykes, "The Kurdish Tribes of the Ottoman Empire," p. 469.
36. Ibid., p. 477.
37. C.J. Edmonds, *Kurds, Turks and Arabs: Politics, Travel and Research in Northern Iraq,* 1919–1925, (London: Oxford University Press, 1957), p. 13.
38. Edmonds, Kurds, Turks and Arabs, p. 14.

the condition that they possess and maintain *namus* (honor), shyness, modesty, sensitiveness, decorum, and a sense of humility.[39]

In order to understand the particular situation and challenges of Kurdish women in Turkey, past and present, it is imperative to elaborate on the topic of *namus* and the discourse around this concept. Familiarity with this term enhances appreciation of the obstacles overcome by Kurdish women in Turkey in their pursuit of cultural, political, and economic advancement. Notably, however, Kurdish women are not the only female population in the Middle East, or the world, whose social code requires adherence to the precepts of *namus* for acceptance within their communities. *Namus* and its tenets are prevalent throughout the Arab-Middle East and North Africa, Muslim-majority societies of Central Asia, and diaspora communities of these regions as well.[40]

Anthropologist Diane E. King translates the term *namus* as honor, but explains that, in the Kurdish context, it can be understood as a form of patrilineal sovereignty.[41] The patrilineal modifier placed before the term sovereignty, as defined by King, implies that an individual woman does not possess her own sovereignty. Rather, a Kurdish woman is a manifestation of *namus* (sovereignty) that actually belongs to the entire family, tribe, and extended community. In the event of a violation of *namus*, either acted out upon a Kurdish woman or brought upon by a woman herself, a loss of honor befalls her entire circle of relations and acquaintances. Subsequently, it is her brother, father, husband, uncle, or male cousins whose duty it is to restore the lost *namus*, customarily by committing an honor killing. King's research indicates that, "without the murder, the lineage… would suffer irreparable harm to its reputation. With the murder this wrong is righted and the lineage is restored to a place of respect in the community."[42] A Kurdish woman, therefore, as gender scholar Deniz Kandiyoti states, is ultimately "the symbolic repository of group identity,"[43] whose transgressions, therefore, are seen as a threat to the integrity of the Kurdish identity and its peoplehood.

---

39. Amir Hassanpour, "The (Re)production of Patriarchy in the Kurdish Language," in Shahrzad Mojab (ed.), *Women of a Non-State Nation: The Kurds* (Costa Mesa, CA: Mazda Publishers, Inc., 2001), p. 230.
40. Diane E. King, "The Personal is Patrilineal: Namus as Sovereignty," *Identities: Global Studies in Culture and Power*, Vol. 15, No. 3 (2008), pp. 317–342.
41. King, "The Personal is Patrilineal," p. 318.
42. Ibid.
43. Deniz Kandiyoti, "Identity and its Discontents: Women and the Nation," *Millenium: Journal of International Studies*, Vol. 20, No. 3 (1991), pp. 429–443.

Key indicators of a woman's *namus* and that of her family are preservation of her virginity and securing early marriage.[44] In order to uphold these values, pre-arranged marriages prevailed as the norm in Kurdish society. With the establishment of the Turkish state in 1923, however, Kurdish women in Turkey technically fell within the jurisdiction of the state and its governing bodies. Turkish Civil Code, codified in 1926, stipulates that a precondition for marriage is the mutual consent of the man and the woman, and grants women equal rights in matters of divorce, child custody, and inheritance. Nevertheless, enforcement of these and other policies pertaining to personal status and family law — to this day — is rare in the Kurdish-populated areas of Turkey.[45]

Over time, Kurdish women and men established practices to circumvent the *namus* code as it applied to marriage without violating it — a tactic that C.J. Edmonds observed in the early twentieth century. He recorded that the women of the Bilbus and Ako tribal confederations, reputed to be "incurably romantic," resorted to abduction *(jin nelh girtin)* and elopement *(rha duw kewtin)* to avoid forced marriages.[46] Historically, agreeing to an elopement or kidnapping was the only act of agency available to Kurdish women in choosing a partner while simultaneously preserving their *namus*. Even today, in the event of a kidnapping/elopement, a couple leaves their village in secret and seeks sanctuary in the custody of a respected and powerful leader who negotiates an appropriate bride price and grants protection to the couple until all offended parties are satisfied. For his services, he excises a *surane* (tax), and determines whether or not another woman from the husband's family, a *berxon*, must replace the loss of the daughter to the elopement/bride kidnapping.[47] (This custom also exists among Arab tribes, particularly those belonging to Shi'i sects.)[48] Thus, one woman's happy ending becomes another's living nightmare, as a probable repercussion of one couple's elopement is a *berdel* arrangement. *Berdel* is the exchange of a woman/bride from the newlywed groom's family to a male in the newlywed bride's family. In a *berdel* arrangement, a practice purportedly now waning in Kurdish society, but nevertheless present (as of 2010), the two couples' fates become tied, as the demise of one marriage

44. Nazand Bagikhani, "Kurdish Women and National Identity," *KurdishMedia.com*, November 8, 2003, accessed April 30, 2011.

45. Pinar Ilkkaracan and Women for Women's Human Rights, "Exploring the Context of Women's Sexuality in Eastern Turkey," *Reproductive Health Matters*, Vol. 6, No. 12, Sexuality (November 1998), pp. 66, 70.

46. Edmonds, *Kurds, Turks and Arabs*, p. 225.

47. Hassanpour, "The (Re)production of Patriarchy," p. 247.

48. Najeeba Mohammed, "Iraqi brides pay high price," *ISN ETH Zurich*, March 20, 2007, accessed April 18, 2013.

requires the dissolution of the other in return.[49] Yet another risk a Kurdish woman undertakes when attempting to choose her partner within or outside the confines of the *namus* code is violation of the "prior right of her father's first paternal cousin's to the girl's hand," and ruining her "father's hope for a good bride-price."[50]

As previously mentioned, a Kurdish woman who violates the social code, which is regulated by community norms and not by any codified legal procedures, elicits a response that strives to preserve or reinstate the family's *namus*. Referring back to the Dominican Priest Campanile's observations of Kurdish society in the nineteenth century, he noted that prostitutes discovered in the act of intercourse with customers received the punishment of being placed in a sack and either were thrown into a river or flung from the top of a nearby mountain.[51] It is reasonable to infer that these women were not all necessarily prostitutes, but also women having pre-marital or extra-marital relations, which, as recorded by Mela Mahmud, were forbidden by society and punishable by death.

Today, as well, the loss of virginity prior to marriage is punishable by methods of hanging, shooting, and, more recently, rat poisoning. These violent acts represent the popular modes for committing contemporary honor killings. Sometimes, families frame these crimes as suicides. Or, they insist on justifying the killings as necessary for the restoration of the family's *namus* under the judgmental eyes of traditional Kurdish society.[52]

The "2011 Report on the Eastern and Southeastern Anatolia Region," published by the Human Rights Association (İHD) Diyarbakır Branch, reported that from March 2010 to March 2011, 72 women were murdered under the categories of suspicious deaths, honor killings, domestic violence, and rape. In the same time period, 113 women committed suicide and 73 women attempted to do so, and there were seven recorded cases of women who were forced into prostitution.[53] Human rights organizations that conduct surveys of violence against women — committed by their own families or those of their spouse — note that numbers are likely higher than what they record, as only a fraction of these types of crimes are actually reported.

---

49. Bijoyeta Das, "For Better or Worse, Sister Swapping Persists," *Women's e-News*, March 22, 2010, accessed April 23, 2011.

50. Edmonds, *Kurds, Turks and Arabs*, p. 226.

51. Galletti, "Western Images of Women's Role in Kurdish Society," p. 211.

52. Nikolaj Nielsen, "Honor Killings and Turkey," *Human Rights: The World Affairs Blog Network, Foreign Policy Blogs*, March 28, 2009, accessed April 25, 2011.

53. "72 Women killed in the past year in South East Turkey," *Rojwomen.com*, March 12, 2011, translated by Berna Ozgencil, accessed March 12, 2011.

In the last decade, field research conducted and analyzed by the non-governmental organization, KA-MER Foundation (Kadın Merkezi — Women's Center), indicates that honor killings, or as KA-MER prefers to call them — "killings committed under the guise of honor" — were also committed to cover up inappropriate distribution of goods and cases of incest.[54] Moreover, KA-MER found that Kurdish society maintains certain justifications for permitting honor killings against women who are "headstrong," act wrongfully, talk back, and don't know "their place." Also, while an individual family may want to eschew the practice of honor killing, KA-MER reported that the reason cited for executing a woman accused of violating the *namus* code was often neighborhood pressure.[55] Persistent adherence to the rules of *namus*, in addition to abusing the reasons for invoking an honor killing, have and continue to influence a majority of Kurdish women's personal choices, as well as determine the potentially drastic consequences in the event that she breaks the code, or is simply accused of having done so.

Aside from entering into a family/community-sanctioned marriage, there are other guarantors of keeping a Kurdish woman's *namus* intact. Observing the "behind-the-scenes" role of women in traditional (rural) Kurdish society in Turkey during the late-1980s, Sheri Laizer described the central function of women as bearing children in wedlock and carrying out the tasks of fieldwork, bread baking, and washing.[56] For these Kurdish women, marriage and the tasks circumscribed to the domestic sphere constituted the tenets of the social contract that offered protection from the threat of a blood feud caused by an incident resulting in dishonor, and represented the accepted endeavors that granted a Kurdish woman the respect of the community.[57]

Marriage, however, never entirely exempted a Kurdish woman from the dangers of *namus* violation. For instance, despite the illegality of polygamy under the Turkish Civil Code established in 1926, this practice remains prevalent among the Kurdish communities of Turkey. Often, in the name of protecting or restoring *namus*, circumstances arise in polygamous marriages that make Kurdish women susceptible to domestic violence. For example, in 2006, Dan Bilefsky, a *New York Times* journalist whose work includes many

---

54. KA-MER "Project for the Development of Permanent Methods in the Struggle Against Killings Committed Under the Guise of 'Honor' in the Southeast and East Anatolia Regions 2005 Report: 'Who's to Blame?'," The KA-MER Foundation, translated by Amy Spangler, 2005.

55. Ibid., p. 4.

56. Sheri Laizer, Into Kurdistan: Frontiers under Fire (London and New Jersey: Zed Books, 1991), p. 35–37.

57. Ibid., p. 44.

articles on honor killings in Turkey, found that while the Turkish state does not recognize polygamous marriages and, even further, imams who conduct them are subject to punishment, polygamy remains widespread in the religious and rural Kurdish region of southeastern Anatolia. In Bilefsky's interview of Handan Coskun, the director of a women's center in the Kurdish-populated Işıklar region (just outside of Diyarbakır), she pointed out that women in polygamous marriages represent a high-risk demographic of Kurdish women, as they have no legal status in a polygamous arrangement carried out under a Muslim religious ceremony that has no legal record. Local authorities charged with law enforcement tend to ignore the occurrence of polygamy in the name of respecting tradition. Consequently, in the event that a husband becomes violent in his resentment for a wife he no longer desires, or cannot provide for his wives and children and abandons them, or the woman feels mistreated, or simply wants to leave the marriage, she possesses absolutely no legal recourse and has nowhere to turn.[58]

Islam's Influence on Kurdish Women's Rights in Turkey

In the early-twentieth century Kurdish nationalist movement, Kurds disseminated unsubstantiated generalizations about the liberated status of Kurdish women to distinguish themselves from the Turks. Janet Klein, a scholar of Kurdish history, outlines the arguments of Kurdish nationalist Memduh Selim Beğ, who boasted that unlike the Turks, the Kurds had "'nationalized Islam according to their own needs'…[and] emerged from the process superior to their neighbors." [59] To support his argument, he claimed that among Kurds polygamy and divorce rates were lower, and unlike his Turkish counterparts, the rights of women under Islam were not under attack. Apparently, Memduh Selim Beğ employed this logic to downplay the efforts of "Islamists or those who used the discourse of religious unity to dismiss nationalist claims."[60] Aside from this historical insight, however, literature that focuses exclusively on Islamic praxis and its influence on the rights of Kurdish women in Turkey is sparse. Yet, the practice and influence of Islam and interpretations of Islamic

---

58. Dan Bilefsky, "Isiklar Journal: Polygamy Fosters Culture Clashes (and Regrets) in Turkey," New York Times, July 10, 2006.
59. Klein, "Engendering Nationalism," p. 38.
60. Klein, "Engendering Nationalism," p. 38.

custom represent another important factor in the discussion of Kurdish women in Turkey.

Most scholars of Kurdish history, including Shahrzad Mojab, Martin van Bruinessen, and Amir Hassanpour, mention the relationship between Islam and the status of Kurdish women only in passing. The authors concur that Islam inhibits Kurdish women's freedom of movement, expression, and choice. However, to better understand how Islam affects Kurdish women in Turkey, it is necessary to find sources from the region in question in order to determine whether or not the practice of Islam and its manifestations in daily life contribute to the struggles of Kurdish women.

Helin Unal, a 29-year-old Kurdish woman from Dersim/Tunceli studying psychology in Maryland, argues that it is impossible to ignore Islam's effect on Kurdish women, but it is not the only factor to consider when studying them. "It is true that honor killings and early marriages are done under Islamic rules and morals," but such phenomena are also "caused by a lack of information/ education or conservativeness, etc…" To that effect, she claims, "men who kill their daughter, wife or niece identify themselves as Muslim. Or men who want to marry off their daughters early (while they're 13, 14 years old) generally say, 'our religion orders it'." But, as Unal notes, calling on Islam as a justification for honor killings partly comes from an ignorance of the religion and its laws and is based on the assumption that the practice of honor killings is sanctioned by Islamic law, which it is not.

She also claims that the cultural influence of Islam depends on the locale and access to education. In Helin's experience, Kurdish families who are politically active send their daughters to school. However, "if a Kurdish family is silent toward Kurdish oppression in Turkey and if they follow Islamic rules rigorously, they do not prefer to send their daughter to school."[61]

> "For example, the Adıyaman's provinces' [in south central Turkey] towns are mostly conservative and women are closed to the world. Sometimes we read terrible news about women. For instance, a young girl was buried alive by her grandfather who was a really religious man in Adıyaman-Menzil [in] 2009. In some towns, some religious organizations are strong, and women suffer there."

On the other hand, according to Unal, in cities women have greater access to schools and other resources, as do their family members; all of which diminish conservative-religious influences. Unal comes from an Alevi-Kurdish family and states that in her community women do not necessarily suffer from early

---

61. Helin Unal, e-mail interview, September 7, 2012.

marriages or honor killings. Nevertheless, there is an expectation "to be a classic wife." This is an expectation that she feels is a form of "gender discrimination, too."[62]

A male source, who requested anonymity, claims that traditional Kurdish leaders such as aghas, sheikhs, and imams, who derive their authority from Islam, "have always dominated Kurdish society's religious opinions." According to the informant, "people had no choice other than to obey... false interpretations...of Islam," that, when referring to women, have been adversarial to women's human rights.[63]

> "For example it was forbidden for girls to go to school, only boys could go. Girls could married [sic] only according to their fathers' choice. If they escape to a man she choosed [sic] for marriage it was the reason to kill her (honor killing). It is not allowed for women to go outside alone, rarely they went to bazaar for shopping, they have no right to speak in family issues [and the] last [final] decision is [the] husband's."[64]

For this informant, these dictates directly conflict with the fact that Islam "sees woman whether single or married as an individual in her own right. She has the right to buy and sell, give gifts and charity, and may spend her money as she pleases. A marriage dowry is given by the groom to the bride for her own personal use and she keeps her own family name rather than taking her husband's."[65] Overall, it appears that the constraints on women put forth by age-old social, cultural, and religious customs of Kurdish communities continue to dictate the reality of the majority of Kurdish women in Turkey today. Many Kurdish women remain unable to make their own decisions regarding sexuality or marriage, education and professional paths, and relegate these important choices to the male members of their families.[66] In the case of Kurdish women in Turkey, while physically located in a mostly modern state with mechanisms in place that are meant to provide women with recourse and opportunity outside the scope of traditional society, the cultural infrastructure of Kurdish society remains largely intact.

---

62. Helin Unal, e-mail interview, September 7, 2012.
63. Anonymous, e-mail interview, September 28, 2012.
64. Ibid.
65. Ibid.
66. Steven Argue, "Kurdish Culture, Repression, Women's Rights, and Resistance," June 12, 2007, accessed April 30, 2011.

Chapter 2

Prominent Women in Kurdish History

In striking contrast to the image of Kurdish women being sold into marriage and murdered for exercising personal choice in matters of the heart and mind, there is also a rich history of influential, powerful Kurdish women. A common title used to identify these exceptional cases in Kurdish women's history is "Khanum," a deferential term referring to a woman who acts as a leader; a woman who acts as head of the household in her husband's absence; a widowed woman; the female head of a tribe (sheikha); or colloquially used by a husband to be polite to his wife.[67] It is imperative to note, however, that prior to the 1980s and the re-articulation of a Kurdish nation-building movement in Turkey, only particular circumstances enabled a Kurdish woman to transcend the boundaries imposed upon her gender and the functions delegated to women as mothers and daughters, i.e. as sources of reproduction and domestic labor. Historically, women who were able to rise to positions of power were the daughters, cousins, and wives of notables, emirs, and wazirs. Toward the late nineteenth and into the early twentieth century, they were also the daughters, wives, cousins, and sisters of Kurdish intellectuals and nationalists.

Chronicles of Kurdish Women from the Seventeenth to Nineteenth Centuries

Early evidence of these claims is found in the writings of the Ottoman traveler Evliya Chelebi, who authored *Book of Travels* in the seventeenth century. According to Chelebi, in Shahrizur (in today's Iraq), customary law *(qanunname)* contained provisions allowing succession to power by daughters and wives. He observed that it was a common enough occurrence to extrapolate that the Kurds generally accepted this custom.[68] In fact, Chelebi came into direct contact with

---

67. Anonymous, Personal Interview, March 20, 2011.
68. Martin van Bruinessen, "From Adela Khanum to Leyla Zana: Women as Political Leaders in Kurdish History," in Shahrzad Mojab (ed.), *Women of a Non-State Nation: The Kurds* (Costa Mesa, CA: Mazda Publishers, Inc., 2001), p. 98.

one of these Kurdish women, Khanzade Sultan. Khanzade, Kurdish for "house of generosity," was the wife of Suleiman, governor of the Soran Emirate (presently the Erbil Governate),[69] and during the reign of Sultan Murad IV (1623–1640), she ruled over the dual principality of Harir and Soran (east and northeast of Erbil in Iraq), commanding 12,000 foot soldiers and 10,000 mounted archers.[70] Awat Baker, Liaison Officer to International Organizations, Department of Foreign Relations, Kurdistan Regional Government of Iraq (KRG) stated, "According to local stories, Sulaiman Beğ differed with the Baghdad government at the time for administrative reasons, and when he went to Baghdad to resolve those differences, he was (not unusually) arrested and imprisoned. There were also internal conflicts with Alababanyen who ruled Sulaymaniyah."[71] Suleiman Beğ did not return from Baghdad and, in fact, met his untimely death in an accident after which Khanzade Sultan took over her husband's position. In a time of internal strife and unrest, she rehabilitated several mosques, built fortifications, and restored security.

In 2000, a Kurdish sculptor by the name of Barzan Ali created a sculpture of Khanzade Sultan, which was installed in the Harir District of the Erbil Province. The sculpture was commissioned to immortalize Khanzade Sultan for the Kurdish people and Kurdish history. Baker cites Khanzade Sultan "as one of the most famous, brave and the most brilliant Kurdish women."[72]

Mirella Galletti contends that the first individual to draw attention to the prominent role held by certain women in Kurdish society was Pietro Della Valle. Della Valle was a renowned Italian traveler of the seventeenth century. His written works, dating back to 1667, mention unveiled women who freely talked to men, both natives and foreigners. In particular, he describes a lady called "Chanun [sic] Sultan," who owned lands and received guests in the absence of her husband "'while he was away serving the king.'"[73]

Another prominent Kurdish woman from the seventeenth century was Asenath Barzani (1590–1670), a Kurdish-Jewish woman from today's Mosul, Iraq.[74] Her father was Rabbi Shmuel b. Netanel Ha-Levi, a highly respected

---

69. Nzibari, "The Iraqi Kurdish Prinicipalities," *Kurdish Musings — No Friends but the Mountains*, March 15, 2012, accessed May 8, 2013.
70. Martin van Bruinessen, "From Adela Khanum to Leyla Zana," p. 99.
71. Awat Baker, Liaison Officer to International Organizations, Department of Foreign Relations, Kurdistan Regional Government of Iraq (KRG), E-mail interview, May 7, 2013.
72. Baker, E-mail Interview, May 7, 2013.
73. Galletti, "Western Images of Women's Role in Kurdish Society," p. 210.
74. "Asnat Barzani, Asenath Barzani 1590–1670 CE," *Womenphilosophers.com*, accessed January 22, 2012.

Jewish scholar and mystic.[75] He was also known by the name of Samuel Barzani (ca. 1630) and reportedly founded several religious schools and seminaries in the Kurdish-speaking areas of today's Iraq, including a well-respected yeshiva in Mosul.[76] According to the research of Avraham Gross and Renee Levine Melammed, Asenath's father had no sons and thus trained his daughter to be a rabbinic scholar instead. When it came time for Asenath to marry, her father arranged a match between his daughter and one of his most promising students, Rabbi Jacob Mizrahi. Apparently, the marriage occurred only after Mizrahi agreed to the stipulations that Asenath would never have to spend her time on housework and, in her capacity as an accomplished Torah scholar, would be able to tutor yeshiva students.[77] After her father passed away, and her husband's sudden demise shortly thereafter, Asenath became the head of the Mosul yeshiva. She is remembered as an accomplished *tanna'it* (Torah scholar), a poetess, and the first woman rabbi in Jewish history.[78] "Asenath's Petition" is one of her few, still extant written works and is an "allegorical plea" for financial support of her yeshiva, where, in addition to serving as its head instructor, she often struggled to replenish its dwindling funds throughout her years as the yeshiva's director.[79]

Although Asenath Barzani was a Kurdish-Jewish figure, in recent years, her biography has become a valuable part of Kurdish women's history. Her story is said to be the oldest record of the role of Kurdish women in history. According to a blog called *Kurdistan's Women*, "Asenath Barzani proves the role of Kurdish women in society centuries ago. Her story as a women [sic] philosopher will be remembered by Kurdish women of this century and the future generations."[80] In further efforts to legitimize the use of her story, an article published by the online news service *Kurd Net* claims that Asenath Barzani "was not only famous among the Jewish community but across the region and among the Kurds,"

75. Renee Levine Melammed, "Asnat Barazani," Jewish Women's Archive, *Jewish Women: A Comprehensive Historical Encyclopedia,* accessed January 16, 2012.
76. Sargis Mamikonian, "Israel and the Kurds (1949–1990)," *Iran and the Caucasus,* Vol. 9, No. 2 (2005), p. 384.
77. Melammed, "Asnat Barazani," Jewish Women's Archive.
78. Avraham Gross, *Pious and Rebellious: Jewish Women in Medieval Europe* (Walthan, MASS: Brandeis University Press, 2004), p. 163.
79. Shirley Kaufman, Galit Hasan-Rokem, and Tamar S. Hess, "Asenath's Petition," from *The Defiant Muse: Hebrew Feminist Poems from Antiquity: A Bilingual Anthology,* The Helen Rose Scheuer Jewish Women's Series (New York: The Feminist Press at City University of New York, 1999), p. 67.
80. Aryan Akrayi, "Asenath Barzani," *Kurdistan's Women Blog,* April 9, 2008, accessed January 29, 2012.

and especially in Amadiya, Iraq, where people came to her for cures to various ailments.[81]

From the nineteenth century, an example of an influential Kurdish woman is Kara Fatima Khanum (Black Lady Fatima), a female chieftain of a Kurdish tribe from Marash (present-day Kahramanmaraş in southeastern Turkey), whose reign reportedly spanned the 1850s.[82] Acting as the leader of one of the largest tribes in Eastern Anatolia, she replaced her husband after his imprisonment and sought to win the favor of the Ottoman sultan so he would free her husband.[83] At the beginning of the Crimean War between the Ottoman Empire and the Russian Empire in 1853, Kara Fatima, chaperoned by her brother, journeyed to Constantinople with 300 warriors on horseback to request an audience with the padişah to show support and offer assistance. According to a German observer, Kara Fatima, who showed up for the war wearing men's garb, had a "manly look."[84] *The Illustrated London News* also documented her activities in its April 22, 1854 edition, which featured the headline "Lioness of Kurdistan."[85] It is also written that Kara Fatima Khanum fought side-by-side with men to defend the City of Erzurum in the Ottoman-Russian War of 1878. It is claimed that she lost many men in the battle, but held her ground and kept the city from the Russians — the event for which she became a legend.[86]

Prominent Kurdish Women of the Early-Twentieth Century

E. B. Soane (1881–1923), a British officer who traveled the areas of today's Iraq, Iran, and Turkey from the early 1900s through approximately 1920, provides one of the most extensive accounts of a ruling Kurdish woman. Disguised as a Persian and claiming to be a traveling scribe and merchant, Soane was employed by the beloved and renowned Adela Khanum (d. 1924),[87] the Kurdish wife of Uthman Paşa, the Ottoman government's appointee as governor *(qa'immaqam)*

81. "Kurdish Asenath Barzani, The first Jewish woman in history to become a Rubbi [*sic*]," *Kurd Net*, September 13, 2010, accessed January 23, 2012.

82. Van Bruinessen, "From Adela Khanum to Leyla Zana," p. 99.

83. Ibid.

84. Galletti, "Western Images of the Woman's Role in Kurdish Society," p. 215.

85. Rohat Alakom, "Kurdish Women in Constantinople at the Beginning of the Twentieth Century," in Shahrzad Mojab (ed.), *Women of a Non-State Nation: The Kurds* (Costa Mesa, CA: Mazda Publishers, Inc., 2001), pp. 54–55.

86. International Free Women's Foundation, *Psychological Trauma*, p. 25.

87. Galletti, "Western Images of the Woman's Role in Kurdish Society," p. 216.

of the district of Shahrizur. In his chronicles, *To Mesopotamia and Kurdistan in Disguise*, Soane described Adela Khanum as a "woman unique in Islam, in the power she possesses, and the efficacy with which she uses the weapons in her hands."[88] Soane, who had taken on the alias of Ghulam Husain,[89] recounted how, during the regular absences of Lady Adela's husband, she gradually accumulated official power. In this capacity, she built a prison, instituted a court of justice and designated herself as its president, and "so consolidated her own power that the Paşa, when he was at Halabja, spent his time smoking a water pipe, building new baths, and carrying out local improvements while his wife ruled."[90]

According to C.J. Edmonds, at the time of the British occupation of Iraq (1914–1918), Adela Khanum was a widow but remained "the uncrowned queen of Shahrizur." During the 1919 rebellion led by Sheikh Mahmud against the British, she proved to be "a staunch supporter of the administration, which recognized and decorated her with the high Indian title of Khan Bahadur."[91] Evidently, Adela Khanum was not interested in the British-bestowed title, but it nevertheless indicated the level of influence she wielded over the men and resources under her domain. When Edmonds came across Adela Khanum on a visit to Halabja in 1922, he noted that although her son, Ahmed Beğ, held title to power, she clearly exercised her influence through him.[92]

During the same time period, Hafsa Khan [*sic*] (1881–1953),[93] a cousin of the renowned Sheikh Mahmud, allegedly saved her kinsman from death. When the British were present in Iraq, she was put in charge of imprisoning British administrators and using them as bargaining chips in negotiations.[94] In 1930, Hafsa Khan continued to play a prominent role in nationalist politics "when she sent a petition to the League of Nations protesting the violation of Kurdish national rights in Iraq," that helped to establish the Kurdish Republic of Iran in 1946, and invested her personal wealth in providing education to Kurdish women.[95]

C.J. Edmonds noted that among ruling Kurdish families in the 1920s and 1930s, it was "quite common for strong-minded women to come forward and

88. E.B. Soane, *To Mesopotamia and Kurdistan in Disguise*, Second Edition (London: J. Murray, 1926), p. 216.
89. Edmonds, *Kurds, Turks and Arabs*, p. 150.
90. Soane, *To Mesopotamia and Kurdistan*, p. 219.
91. Edmonds, *Kurds, Turks and Arabs*, p. 50.
92. Ibid., p. 157.
93. Mojab, "Nationalism and Feminism: The Case of Kurdistan," p. 70.
94. Hansen, *The Kurdish Woman's Life*, p. 9.
95. Mojab, "Nationalism and Feminism: The Case of Kurdistan," p. 70.

play an important part in tribal politics."[96] As such, he wrote of Fatima Khanum, who came from outside Rawanduz (in today's Iraq), and administered eight villages in the wake of her husband's death. Allegedly, her villages chose her to vote on their behalf at parliamentary elections despite a law that stated only men could do so.[97] He also told of Agha Zin, "a very masterful lady," who was the wife of Surk Agha. Also known as "Madam Agha," Agha Zin was younger than her "foolish husband and conducted all business connected to the maintenance of the political balance of power in the remote valley where Ranya village [in Northern Iraq] was located." Apparently, in the aftermath of her husband's murder, Agha Zin herself prosecuted the blood feud "with greatest vigour until she had taken full vengeance that tribal honor required."[98]

Edmonds also shared the tale of Faqê Marif, a "quaint character known by the man's name of Faqê," who was really a 25-year-old woman and a professional jester, who wandered "guest house to guest house mixing freely with men by day, returning to the women's quarters by night."[99] Edmonds claimed that when he asked her why she did not marry she replied, "simply that it was not in her nature to do."[100]

The "Woman Question" and the Kurdish-Ottoman Nationalist Movement (1913–1922)

According to historian Janet Klein, urban Kurdish women made their debut on the stage of nationalist Kurdish-Ottoman politics in 1913. During this year, a Kurdish writer informed the readers of his publication, *Kurdish Press*, that the entire West and parts of the East were preoccupied with the "woman question."[101] In the context of a rising nationalist consciousness, the "woman question" was presented as a social issue whose solution would contribute elements of progress, modernity, and prosperity of the pursuit of Kurdish nationhood, as well as help to gain Western sympathy for the Kurdish national cause.[102] In the same year, Ulviye Mevlan, the wife of Mevlanzade Rifat (a Kurdish journalist), supervised the publication of *Woman's World* (*Kadınlar Dünyasi — Monde Féminin*), which touched upon the "woman question" and saw 200 issues go to

---

96. Edmonds, *Kurds, Turks and Arabs*, p. 14.
97. Ibid.
98. Ibid., p. 233.
99. Ibid., p. 234.
100. Ibid.
101. Klein, "En-Gendering Nationalism," p. 25.
102. Ibid., pp. 28–29.

print.[103] The publication became a voice for all Ottoman women, regardless of religion, sect, or ethnic group.[104]

In 1919, the Society for the Advancement of Kurdish Women (Kürd Kadınları Teali Cemiyeti) was founded as a branch of the Society for the Advancement of Kurdistan (Kürdistan Teali Cemiyeti). *Women's World* printed the Society's regulations as a way to advertise itself and enjoin women to participate in the national awakening, which called for education reform, including a literacy campaign and the standardization of Kurdish language.[105] Emine Xanim, the Kurdish granddaughter of Mehmet Ali Paşa of Egypt, served as the head of the Society for the Advancement of Kurdish Women. She regularly corresponded with two Swedish female friends, both well-known progressives on the topic of women's rights.[106]

But despite the handful of women involved in the nationalist movement, Klein argues that the discourse of the "woman question" in the early twentieth century was not so much about women themselves, but instead garnered its importance from men who deemed women as useful and significant symbols for the burgeoning nationalist discourse. As a result, the "woman question" intertwined with other issues, such as culture, religion, the economy, and nationalism.[107] Furthermore, academic and activist Shahrzad Mojab argues that although the Society for the Advancement of Kurdish Women was the first of its kind for the Kurds, the fact that male and female members of Istanbul's Kurdish aristocracy founded the society points to the organization's limited scope and influence and its minimal contribution to the cause of Kurdish women's advancement.[108] In comparison to the activities of Kurdish women today, which include women from across the socio-economic spectrum in politics, journalism, militarism, and so on, both Klein and Mojab's arguments hold true. (This phenomenon appeared elsewhere in the Middle East where men initiated the "emancipation of women.")

---

103. Alakom, "Kurdish Women in Constantinople," p. 58.
104. Ibid.
105. Klein, "En-Gendering Nationalism," pp. 32–34.
106. Alakom, "Kurdish Women in Constantinople," p. 63.
107. Klein, "En-Gendering Nationalism," pp. 25–26.
108. Mojab, "Nationalism and Feminism: The Case of Kurdistan," p. 70.

Kurdish Female Writers and One Negotiator
(an Exception to the Exception)

In the past, Kurdish women were also writers, although both Kurdish men and women were late in composing in their mother tongue. Indeed, Asenath Barzani wrote in the Hebrew-Aramaic dialect spoken by Kurdish Jews. Matsura Kurdistani (1805–1849; a member of the Ardalan aristocracy and married to Khosrow Khan, head of the Kurdish Municipality of Ardalan in today's Iran), who wrote many books in the fields of history, poetry, Islamic thought, and the lives of Kurdish poets, mainly did so in Persian, although she composed a few poems in Kurdish.[109]

In Rohat Alakom's investigation of Kurdish women in Istanbul at the beginning of the twentieth century, he found a handful of letters written by young Kurdish women and published them in the post-World War I Kurdish-Ottoman newspaper *Jîn* (Life).[110] He notes that these women represented the privileged few who attended school or managed to become teachers. Similarly, Hashem Ahmadzadeh's research indicates that although the Kurdish novel emerged in 1935, until the last decade of the twentieth century the genre was entirely dominated by Kurdish men.[111] Unless a Kurdish woman belonged to a prominent family endowed with private wealth, property, and connections to a regional ruling power, few to no opportunities for public involvement or professional development were available to her.

An exception to the rule was Rabi'a, a lower-class woman (notably from an urban, not a rural setting), who became head of the bakers of Sulaimaniyya in the early 1920s. During an economic crisis, she negotiated with the municipality on a fixed price for bread, all the while maintaining "admirable discipline among her colleagues in the craft who were second only to the butchers."[112] Known to give "sage advice," she also exercised "firm control over tradesmen."[113] Perhaps there were other such women, but, as established in the previous chapter, Rabi'a's image is not representative of the majority of Kurdish women.

Regardless of the motives that led to the inclusion of the "woman question" in Kurdish nationalist discourse of the early twentieth century, or the regularity with which an urban or rural Kurdish noblewoman rose to a position of authority, in the aftermath of World War I the political situation of the Kurds

---

109. Hashem Ahamzadeh, "The World of Kurdish Women's Novels," *Iranian Studies*, Vol. 41, No. 5 (December 2008), p. 736, note 28.
110. Alakom, "Kurdish Women in Constantinople," p. 56.
111. Ahamzadeh, "The World of Kurdish Women's Novels," p. 719.
112. Mojab, "Nationalism and Feminism: The Case of Kurdistan," p. 70.
113. Edmonds, *Kurds, Turks and Arabs*, p. 86.

halted further evolution of Kurdish political, social, and cultural reform. With the establishment of the Turkish state and its insistence on a super-imposed, universal, Turkish national-ethnic identity, claiming one's Kurdishness became grounds for the charge of treason. As Kurdish ethnicity was a key aspect of nationalist discourse, the illegalization of defining oneself as a Kurd signaled the abrupt end to developments in a distinctively nationalist direction. Naturally, in this volatile political environment the Kurdish discourse on the "woman question" all but ceased.

Chapter 3

The Partition of Kurdistan:
The Silent Years on the Kurdish
"Woman Question"

On July 18, 1919, British Major E.W.C. Noel wrote a paper titled "Notes on the Kurdish Situation." In the section "Turkish Policy In Regard to the Kurds," the author noted:

> "The Turk… has consistently refused to acknowledge the existence of Kurdish nationality. In all official documents the word Kurdish is eschewed and the word Moslem substituted. The printing of books in Kurdish is prohibited. The Kurdish clubs have been closed, Kurdish agents arrested and in the past many Kurdish nationalists have been secretly put to death…refugees to western vilayets are not allowed to congregate in communities of their own, but should be distributed in small groups among the Turkish population. The object was to Ottomanize the Kurd as rapidly as possible."[114]

In the aftermath of World War I, however, a defeated Ottoman Empire initially surrendered the fate of the Kurds to the Allied Powers. In 1920, Sultan Mehmet VI and the Allied Powers of World War I (the British Empire, France, Italy, and Japan) signed the Treaty of Sèvres. With regard to the Kurds, Article 62 stipulated that six months after the treaty came into force, a commission composed of three members chosen by the British, French, and Italian governments would draft "a scheme of local autonomy" for the predominantly Kurdish areas of the former Ottoman Empire. Article 64 of the Treaty of Sèvres mandated that in the event of the Kurds petitioning the League of Nations for

---

114. B. Destani, ed., *Minorities in the Middle East: Kurdish Communities, 1918-1974*, Vol. 1, 1918–1930, Document 2, Despatch No. 1268/M1743 from Sir A. Calthorpe, High Commissioner, Constantinople, to Earl Curzon of Keddleston, Secretary of State for the Colonies, 23 July 1919, enclosing a paper titled "Notes on the Kurdish Situation," by Major E.W.C. Noel, Constantinople, 18 July 1919, together with paper titled "Mesopotamia: British Relations with Kurdistan" by the Political Department, India Office, 27 August 1919 [FO608/95], (Archive Editions Ltd., 2006), p. 86.

independent statehood within one year, should the international body find
Kurdistan suitable for independence, Turkey would renounce all rights and
claims of ownership over that territory.[115]

Shortly thereafter, however, Mustafa Kemal Atatürk, the founder of modern
Turkey, successfully led his troops to reoccupy the territory partitioned by the
Allied Powers. The now-Turkish segment of Kurdistan fell under Atatürk's
authority. Negotiations between Atatürk and the Allied Powers, who decided to
support Atatürk's strong-arm approach, resulted in the 1923 Treaty of Lausanne,
which reestablished "complete and undivided Turkish sovereignty" over nearly
all the territories that comprise modern-day Turkey and canceled all articles
pertaining to the potential autonomy of the Kurds in the Treaty of Sèvres.[116]
According to Turkish sociologist I. Beşikçi, the signing of the Treaty of Lausanne
informally condoned the implementation of Atatürk's divide-and-rule policies
against the Kurds, and allowed the leader to forcefully instate a new, narrowly-
defined nationalism named after the leader himself: "Kemalism."[117]

At first, Kurdish politicians accepted their absorption into the new
Turkish state based upon Article 88 of the 1924 constitution, which "…laid the
groundwork for a potentially inclusive understanding of national identity by
acknowledging the existence of racial variety,"[118] and so they complied with
Atatürk's plans. However, the wider Kurdish response to the perception of
lost autonomy was continued rebellion led by Kurdish landlords, tribal chiefs,
sheikhs, and urban-based intellectuals (Kurdish nationalists). With the outbreak
of the Kurdish-led Sheikh Said Rebellion of 1925, Turkish leaders began to view
"the presence of a 'Kurdish people' within Turkey's border as a clear territorial
threat,"[119] which led to the rapid deterioration of Kurdish-Turkish relations.

In response to the Kurdish challenge, Atatürk's military carried out mass
executions, village destructions, and deportations.[120] In 1925, 35 percent of
Turkey's state budget was used to suppress the Sheikh Said Revolt, followed by
the 1930 Dersim Revolt, and the Mount Ararat Revolt that spanned from 1936 to

---

115. "The Treaty of Sèvres, 1920, Section III, Articles 62–64," The Treaties of Peace
     1919–23, Vol. 2, (New York: The Carnegie Endowment for Peace, 1924), accessed on
     October 1, 2011.
116. Bernard Lewis, The Emergence of Modern Turkey, Second Edition (London: Oxford
     University Press, 1969 reprint), p. 255.
117. International Free Women's Foundation, Psychological Trauma, p. 27.
118. Nicole F. Watts, "Allies and Enemies: Pro-Kurdish Parties in Turkish Politics, 1990-
     94," International Journal of Middle East Studies, Vol. 31, No. 4 (November 1999), pp.
     631–656.
119. Watts, "Pro-Kurdish Parties," p. 634.
120. International Free Women's Foundation, Psychological Trauma, p. 27.

1938.[121] As early as 1925, Atatürk imposed the Law for the Maintenance of Public Order, which broadly authorized military suppression of any form of perceived opposition.[122] At the same time, Atatürk oversaw the vigorous enforcement of a canon of laws that sought to physically break up Kurdish communities, to prevent further Kurdish political mobilization, and to erase Kurdish history and identity. Kurdish names of cities in southeastern Turkey were replaced with Turkish names, and the Kurdish language became practically banned from use.[123]

In 1934, the Turkish National Assembly passed the İskan Kanunu (Settlement Act) that aimed to change the demographics of Southeast Anatolia based on ethnic considerations and prohibited settlement in certain regions — mostly the Kurdish ones. Implementation of the İskan Kanunu began in Dersim. Existing Kurdish villages were dismantled and the population forcibly removed and resettled in Western Turkey. The goal of the policy was to displace Kurds so as to prevent political organization that would lead to upheaval against the Turkish government, however, the official reasons given for the depopulation of Ağri, Dersim, Van, Kars, the southern part of Diyarbakır, Bingöl, Bitlis, and Muş were out of "hygienic, economic, cultural, military, and security concerns."[124]

Starting in May 1932, denial of Kurdish identity became Turkish state policy when the Kurds of Turkey "were classified as 'Mountain Turks'," referring to "a group of people who had forgotten their own Turkish identity and roots."[125] By 1936, General Abdullah Alpdoğan, the military governor of Tunceli (formerly Dersim), reiterated the nonexistence of Kurdish people when he announced that Kurdish people did not exist as a race, but rather these people were Turkish natives residing in the mountains.[126] Hussein Tahiri cites the beginning of the "Mountain Turk" nomenclature for the Kurds of Turkey following the

121. Metin Yüksel, "The Encounter of Kurdish Women with Nationalism in Turkey," *Middle Eastern Studies*, Vol. 42, No. 5 (July 2006), pp. 777–802.
122. Kevin McKiernan, *The Kurds: A People in Search of a Homeland* (New York: St. Martin's Press, 2006), p. 93.
123. Aliza Marcus, *Blood and Belief: the PKK and the Kurdish Fight for Independence* (New York and London: New York University Press, 2007), p. 18.
124. International Free Women's Foundation, *Psychological Trauma*, p. 28.
125. Hay Eytan Cohen Yanarocak, "A Nonviolent Kurdish Political Movement in Turkey," in Ofra Bengio (ed.), *Kurdish Awakening: Nation Building in a Fragmented Homeland* (Austin: University of Texas Press, 2014), p. 138.
126. McKiernan, *The Kurds: A People in Search of a Homeland*, p. 94.

suppression of the 1938 Dersim Revolt.[127] Successive administrations followed suit, denying the Kurds their ethno-national identity, until 1991.[128]

Turkey's Use of Kurdish Women as a Weapon

According to eyewitness accounts, the siege of Dersim in 1938, the goal of which was to squash the rebellion started by Seyd Riza in 1936, resulted in thousands of casualties, mass rapes, and extensive violence against women. In addition to quashing the manpower behind the resistance, the logic of the Turkish army, it was claimed, was to exploit the *namus* code of the Kurdish people by sexually abusing its women, thereby weakening the Kurdish people's morale and resolve. Reportedly, thousands of women and girls committed suicide to avoid such a fate, throwing themselves from high rocks into the Munzur River (located in the Munzur Valley of the Tunceli/Dersim Province in eastern Anatolia).[129]

Although Kurdish political activity did not completely come to a halt, Mojab claims that, aside from the efforts of Hafsa Khan (refer to Chapter Two), there is no evidence that women participated in the occasional uprisings of the decades that succeeded the revolts of the 1920s and 1930s.[130] However, it is worth mentioning that PKK literature remembers three women as heroes from this period of unrest: Zarife, who participated in the Kocgiri uprising (1920-21), Perihan in the uprising of Diyarbakır, and Bese in the Dersim Rebellion of 1937.[131]

Between the 1925 Şark Islahat Planı (Şark Reform Plan, which banned the use of Kurdish in public) and the 1934 Law for the Maintenance of Public Order (İskan Kanunu), Turkish authorities largely succeeded in suppressing public, political expression of Kurdishness.[132] Furthermore, forcibly re-populating the western portion of the country with Kurds turned the Kurdish areas of Turkey, in the east and southeast, into the poorest, least developed areas of the country, where systematic marginalization, assimilation, and repression characterized daily existence.[133] The Turkish government did not allocate funds to the

---

127. Hussein Tahiri, "The Kurdish Republic of 1946," in Ofra Bengio (ed.), *Kurdish Awakening: Nation Building in a Fragmented Homeland* (Austin: University of Texas Press, 2014), p. 254.
128. McKiernan, *The Kurds: A People in Search of a Homeland*, p. 94.
129. International Free Women's Foundation, *Psychological Trauma* , p. 28.
130. Mojab, "Nationalism and Feminism: The Case of Kurdistan," p. 70.
131. International Free Women's Movement, *Psychological Trauma*, p. 28.
132. Ibid., p. 29.
133. Amir Hassanpour, "The Kurdish Experience," *Middle East Report*, No. 189 (July–August 1994), p. 7.

infrastructure of this part of the country, which either left Kurds to languish in sub-par conditions, or to seek opportunity in other parts of the country. By 1939, the Turkish authorities believed they had solved the Kurdish "problem" and, to reinforce this conclusion, deported hundreds of thousands of Kurds to western Turkey in order to discourage any further political organizing.[134] Consequently, the years between 1938 and 1968 came to be known as the "silent decades" of the Kurdish plight.[135]

Unintended Consequences: Planting the Seeds of Resistance

Overall, the partition of Kurdistan and the policies implemented to overcome opposition to partition were detrimental to the lives of Turkey's Kurdish women. Additionally, the dispersal and subsequent dissolution of the Ottoman Empire's Kurdish intelligentsia, which had initiated the discourse on the Kurdish "woman question," made Kurdish women a particularly vulnerable population in Turkey. Nevertheless, the unintended consequences of these policies eventually contributed to the capabilities that would strengthen Kurdish women's role in the current Kurdish ethno-national movement in Turkey.

During the silent decades, sporadic peasant uprisings perpetuated forced migration through "land reforms," resulting in continual, internal displacement of the Kurds. One of the repercussions of these policies included the urbanization of segments of Kurdish society. As both Kurdish men and women traveled to major city centers in Turkey, such as Ankara and Istanbul, a modern, urban, and educated Kurdish class gradually arose. Over the years, rising numbers of Kurdish men and women's access to the urban setting translated into increased education and participation in social, economic, political, and cultural life. The significance of population transfers on Kurdish society, which resulted in the dislocation of the traditional intelligentsia (i.e., the ulema and educated landed notables), and the urbanization of rural Kurds who were partially integrated into the Turkish state would only be apparent, though, once the Kurdish nationalist movement resurfaced in the late 1960s.[136]

Unquestionably, confinement in a repressive atmosphere, enforced by the prohibition of Kurdish language and identity, exacerbated by family

---

134. Ibid., p. 3.
135. Ali Kemal Özcan, *Turkey's Kurds: A Theoretical Analysis of the PKK and Abdullah Öcalan* (London and New York: Routledge, Taylor & Francis Group, 2006), p. 60.
136. Hassanpour, "The Kurdish Experience," p. 5.

separation — either by force of the Turkish authorities or out of necessity to search for a livelihood — weakened Kurdish society as a whole. However, another unforeseen consequence of these policies materialized from the 1940s to the late 1960s. Although the majority of Turkey's Kurds located in rural areas became further impoverished and dislocated from the rest of their society, scholars F. Şenpinar and M. Mies argue that policies of internal displacement created circumstances which resulted in a fascinating outcome for rural Kurdish women, which also became apparent in the 1960s and 1970s. In the power vacuum left by displaced men (by force or by necessity), a space opened for rural women to exercise control and agency previously unavailable to them. Şenpinar and Mies claim that, in this period of time, women who remained in villages became responsible for independent decision-making regarding family matters and farming issues, which improved their self-esteem.[137] According to this argument, the "feminization of agriculture" in parts of Kurdish society, an unintended consequence of Turkish policy meant to weaken Kurdish society, resulted in the unlikely empowerment of rural Kurdish women.

---

137. International Free Women's Foundation, *Psychological Trauma*, p. 31.

Chapter 4

The Double Oppression of the Kurdish Women of Turkey

Throughout history, the control and manipulation of women's appearance and behavior has been a driving factor in the creation of cultural identity. Susan McDonald, an international human rights lawyer, notes that throughout the world, women are designated as the keepers of tradition because women strengthen and fortify the community's sense of common history and culture.[138] According to anthropologist Carole Nagengast, in the modern state, the concept of culture "circumscribes women's lives in deeply symbolic as well as immediately real and concrete ways. Through their clothing, body embellishments, and demeanor, women and girls...are repositories and guardians of cultural meanings..."[139] Logically then, the most efficient method to form, alter, preserve, or damage a nation's identity, its collective understanding, and its historic legacy is to focus on the status and role of the women falling under its jurisdiction. Unfortunately for women, this approach to nation building strips women of personal and political agency. As Nagengast points out, in the context of nation or nation-state building, women become viewed as the "angels of culture," a phenomenon which assigns them a second class status because they are viewed as aspects — as opposed to agents — of society that must be protected from themselves and the outside world.[140] In the aftermath of the partition of Kurdistan, both Atatürk and traditional Kurdish leaders, in part, sought to define and defy the Turkish nation through the vehicle of women.

Early efforts to create a national identity in Turkey, and the opposing attempts to maintain a distinctive Kurdish one, objectified women as symbols of cultural identity rather than full members of either respective society. The outcome of this perception of Kurdish women's national-cultural function and the policies that enforced it (both formal and informal) was a twofold negative effect,

---

138. Susan McDonald, "Kurdish Women and Self-Determination: A Feminist Approach to International Law," in Shahrzad Mojab (ed.), *Women of a Non-State Nation: The Kurds* (Costa Mesa, CA: Mazda Publishers, Inc., 2001), p. 146.

139. Carole Nagengast, "Women, Minorities, and Indigenous Peoples: Universalism and Cultural Relativity," *Journal of Anthropological Research*, Vol. 53, No. 3, Universal Human Rights versus Cultural Relativity (Autumn 1997), pp. 349–369.

140. Ibid., p. 359.

characterized by isolation within their own community and marginalization vis-à-vis the Turkish nation-building project. To the present day, many Kurdish families refuse to send their daughters to school, "arguing that if they cannot be educated in Kurdish they will not be able to transmit the Kurdish language to their children in the future."[141]

Furthermore, in the period under discussion Kurdish women have served as a means by which the Turkish authorities attempt to suppress the ethno-national struggle. Throughout the conflict the military, police, and anti-terror units have engaged in systematic sexual torture of Kurdish women in order to demoralize the Kurdish people. Well aware of the socio-cultural tenet of *namus* and the ramifications of its breach (as explained in Chapter Three), state-perpetrated violation of the honor concept continues. Aside from the physical and psychological abuse of the victims, Kurdish women suffer doubly when, out of fear of retaliation, ostracism, forced marriage, or the knowledge that there is a minimal chance for justice, many women still remain silent in the face of this violence.[142]

Kemalism on Women: The Dos and Don'ts

With the establishment of Kemalist Turkey, a number of expedient measures were implemented to catalyze the top-down modernization and secularization of the country, many of which directly affected women. In 1926, Turkey adopted the Swiss Civil Code, which abolished polygamy and banned the veil; outlawed child marriages by imposing a minimum legal age; recognized women as legal equals to men in the areas of bearing witness in a court of law and inheriting and maintaining property; and granted women the right to choose their spouse, initiate divorce, and to retain child custody even after divorce. By 1930 and 1934, women were granted the right to vote in municipal and national elections, respectively.[143]

On paper, female citizens of Turkey appeared to receive new opportunities to increase their presence and equal status in the public sphere. Women were encouraged to pursue an education and enter the workforce at the professional level as well. Women who were willing to comply with the Kemalist doctrine of women's liberation and to embody the terms that characterized the new Turkish

---

141. Bernard, "Women and the Kurdish Movement in Turkey," *The WVoice*, Vol. 2, No. 4, May 8, 2014, p. 4.

142. "Turkey: End sexual violence against women in custody!," *Amnesty International*, February 26, 2003, EUR 44/006/2003, p. 5.

143. Yüksel, "The Encounter of Kurdish Women," p. 781.

female-cultural symbol that Atatürk wanted (that is, an outwardly modernized, western female-cultural symbol with a role in the public sphere that did not complain about gender inequality in the private sphere), were able to exercise their new rights and to gradually enjoy success in realms of professional and public experience previously available only to men. Simultaneously, however, as mentioned in the previous chapter, the Kemalist agenda's paramount priority was to construct a cohesive nation-state that was ethnically, linguistically, and culturally homogeneous from "the remnants of the Ottoman Empire, which was a multi-ethnic, multi-linguistic and multi-cultural entity."[144] Ultimately, with regard to women, "the authoritarian Kemalist state-promoted feminism" rendered women "passive receivers of 'progressive' state policies."[145]

Moreover, in the context of the conflict between the Kurds and Turkey — a state that categorically denied Kurdish ethnic identity, language, and culture, and enforced legislation to realize these objectives — Kurdish women's knowledge of women's rights promotion and reform policies were negligible, and their access to these rights more limited still. Kurdish women were Kurds first. Consequently, even if a Kurdish woman wanted to pursue these newly gained rights, her place in Kurdish society and the corresponding restraints on her movement and behavior meant these opportunities were either non-existent or inaccessible to her.

Another principal factor that isolated Kurdish women from the potential advantage of Turkish gender policy was traditional Kurdish leaders' grasp on local authority, and the Turkish state's role in coopting these leaders and their power. Although a large segment of Kurdish leadership and, particularly, the nationalist factions rejected the Turkish state, there were others who were willing to cooperate with Atatürk for the right price and promises. Even after the suppression of Kurdish rebellions, Jenny White's research shows that the strength of traditional Kurdish forces (aghas, landowners, religious sheikhs, and tribal leaders), continued to act as formidable opponents to the Turkish state.[146] To overcome threats to the state's integrity springing from these Kurdish factions, Turkish authorities struck a bargain with parties who were willing to compromise in exchange for policing Kurdish opposition. As long as defiance against the state and its nation-building process ceased, the ways in which these Kurdish leaders officiated their respective communities were inconsequential to the Turkish rulers.

---

144. Ibid., p. 777.
145. Bernard, "Women and the Kurdish Movement in Turkey," *The WVoice*, Vol. 2, No. 4, May 8, 2014, p. 3.
146. Yüksel, "The Encounter of Kurdish Women," p. 787.

Evidence of this dynamic appears in the notes of British Diplomat D. Scott-Fox, recorded after his travels to Van and its surrounding areas as early as 1951. According to Scott-Fox's dispatch, in the towns he visited near Van, most women were veiled, some of them fully, and polygamy was noticeably practiced throughout Turkey.[147] Out of the purview of the Turkish authorities and left to the local rule of traditional power holders, Kurdish social customs prevailed. Women's main function in society remained domestic, raising children, and tending the land, which, to some extent, was an intentional tactic to resist modernization and secularization (central characteristics of the new national-Turkish identity). Thus, at the same time that populations of women in Turkey were gaining access to education, employment opportunities, and representation in the Turkish government (albeit nominal), Kurdish women, particularly in the Southeast, were trapped in a society — in part by its own volition — frozen in time.

Disparities in Development and Turning a Blind Eye

Turkey's concentration of industrial development and infrastructure expansion in the country's western region resulted in the economic migration of the mostly male labor force and fortified a pattern of neglect of rural Kurdish areas.[148] Kurdish women became further disadvantaged due to a severe lack of schools and limited employment opportunities. If and where there were chances for advancement, community leaders opposed modernization measures seen as interfering with Kurdish custom, leaving the majority of Kurdish women to suffer in silence. Kurdish women were also excluded from opportunities to learn the Turkish language, whereas Kurdish men (although equally disenfranchised) were required to serve in the Turkish army, where they learned the language and therefore benefited from greater economic and educational opportunities. Primarily, then, the state interfered with the Kurds when they dared to be Kurdish, and recused itself from the Kurds' affairs in one of the few realms of sovereignty they maintained: the control over Kurdish women.

---

147. B. Destani (ed.), *Minorities in the Middle East: Kurdish Communities, 1918–1974*, Vol. 3, 1941–1967, Document 71, Confidential despatch [*sic*] No. 117 (1631/4/51), from Mr. D. Scott-Fox, British Embassy, Ankara, to Mr. H. Morrison, Foreign Office, 21 May 1951, enclosing a confidential report by Mr. Arthur, Second Secretary at Ankara Embassy, undated title "A tour in South East Anatolia during April 1951," [FO248/1523], p. 275.

148. International Free Women's Foundation, *Psychological Trauma*, p. 30.

Perhaps the most explicit example of this situation is illustrated by the fact that only in 2004 did an amendment to the Turkish Penal Code render crimes against women, such as honor killings, to be litigated within the framework of crimes against humanity.[149] Although honor killings occur throughout Turkey among many of its ethnic groups, it is particularly pronounced in conservative Kurdish families in the Southeast or among migrants from the southeast living in large cities.[150] Prior to 2004, Article 59 of the Turkish Penal Code permitted judges to exercise discretion in identifying extenuating circumstances that provided for the mitigation of a sentence in an honor killing case. For example, a judge could decide to commute a life sentence to 30-years imprisonment, citing "cultural practice" as the justification for this ruling.[151] While this may be a positive step in the direction of justice for what the KA-MER Foundation terms extrajudicial killings, for an honor killing to come to the attention of a judge in a Turkish court, first it has to be reported. Reports authored by human rights organizations which work in Kurdish communities have noted that despite an increase in the reporting of honor killing cases, the majority of these incidents still are not disclosed.

Sexual Violence Committed by the State: the Targeting of Kurdish Women

In the twentieth century conflict between the Kurds and the Turkish state, when the Kurds challenged status quo, the state apparatus targeted Kurdish women in order to suppress resistance. Since the rise of the Kurdish national movement that exploded in the mid-1980s, Kurdish women have been victims of state-sanctioned violence and sexual violence, including torture, abduction, arbitrary arrest, and detention, in the name of state security.[152] Mainly, systematic use of sexual violence has been used by the Turkish authorities against women who have expressed "unacceptable political opinions" and in the presence of

149. Idil Aybars, "Seeking real equality for Turkey's women," *Common Ground News Service*, November 25, 2011, accessed November 25, 2011.

150. Kurdish Human Rights Project (London), "The Increase in Kurdish Women Committing Suicide," a study published by the European Parliament, Policy Department C Citizens' Rights and Constitutional Affairs, Women's Rights and Gender Equality, June 2007, PE 393.248, p. 14.

151. KA-MER, "Who's to Blame?," p. 5.

152. Kurdish Human Rights Project (London), "The Increase in Kurdish Women Committing Suicide," p. 4.

male relatives to force "confessions" to anti-state activities.[153] The overarching function of state-perpetrated sexual violence (against women and men) has been a "cynical" and intentional abuse of the Kurdish concept of honor, a tool with which "state agents can control dissent" by torturing and degrading women to attack "the woman, her family, group, and community."[154]

Eren Kesken, a female-Kurdish human rights lawyer, has been representing Kurdish women abused by the state since the mid-1990s. Kesken discovered her Kurdish ethnicity at the age of 14 when an uncle pulled her aside during a family vacation and revealed this information to her. In 1995 she published an article that included the word "Kurdistan." For this, she received a three-year jail sentence on the claim that she was a member of the PKK. After serving six months in prison, Kesken was set free. Upon her release, she began offering free legal aid to Kurdish women seeking justice from the state. This decision was inspired by her time in prison during which Kesken shared a cell with several other women who were incarcerated on suspicion of PKK involvement. She claims that each woman with whom she spoke had been subject to rape or sexual harassment at the hands of military or police personnel and state Anti-Terror units "for political or non-political reasons." As of 2009, the rampant practice of sexual torture and abuse by state agents was still commonplace. Some of her cases, however, have proven impossible to prosecute due to the fact that some women have been abducted and detained without any record. Presently, Kesken represents hundreds of cases, receiving 20 to 30 new ones each year from both Kurdish women and Turkish women who have been violated by individuals representing state authorities. Of the approximately 200 cases brought against Kesken for separatism, 21 of them were still active in 2009. She still continues her work.[155]

The Kurdish Human Rights Project (KHRP) is an organization that has made bold efforts and some success in exposing, prosecuting, and documenting institutionalized sexual violence against Kurdish women. In December 2003, the KHRP published an observation report documenting a trial involving 405 members of the Turkish Gendarme of the Derik District (in the Mardin Province of southeastern Anatolia) indicted under the Turkish penal code for the torture and rape of a Kurdish woman by the name of Şükran Esen in 1993 and 1994.[156]

---

153. "Turkey: End sexual violence against women in custody!", p. 5.

154. Ibid., p. 12.

155. *Al-Jazeera*, "Witness — Turkey's Hidden Shame," *Al-Jazeera*, a short documentary film, Parts 1 & 2, accessed March 24, 2013.

156. Kurdish Human Rights Project (KHRP), "Trial Observation Report, Turkey's Shame: Sexual Violence Without Redress — the Plight of Kurdish Women," KHRP, December 2003.

The report used this case to demonstrate Turkey's systematic failure to protect Kurdish women (being full citizens of Turkey), or to provide them with adequate recourse to the occurrence of sexual torture and rape at the hands of state authorities. Nevertheless, this form of abuse persists, and the consequences of these experiences continue to hinder the development of Kurdish women in Turkey.

In the ongoing conflict between the Kurds and the state of Turkey, Kurdish women and men have suffered a host of psychological, physical, and spiritual hardships. However, in the past decade, the rising rate of suicide among Kurdish women has led to a number of studies that focus on the specific ways in which women have suffered especially. For Kurdish women in Turkey, the consequences of the conflict, include state-perpetrated sexual violence, increased domestic violence, mental and psychological problems, and honor killings. These crises are compounded by a patriarchal society in which family pressures encourage violated women to remain quiet out of shame, which leads to a lack of acknowledgment of mental and psychological problems. In this volatile environment, Kurdish women lack protection from forced marriages, forced prostitution, polygamy, and domestic and state violence. Furthermore, through a lack of education and language barriers, an ailing economy, unemployment, and a persistent tension between tradition and modernism, many Kurdish women in Turkey continue to suffer in silence.[157]

In the context of an undeclared civil war, Kurdish women are seen as Kurds first (potential enemies of the state) and citizens second. Their inability, "in practical terms, to enjoy their linguistic rights," freedom of association or expression, further contributes to the unlikelihood of their receiving "speedy redress or compensation for the many abuses that they endure,"[158] and makes these violations all the more egregious and frequent. The use of Kurdish women as a weapon against their own people for the purpose of stifling an ethno-national movement has perpetuated the disenfranchisement and alienation of a majority of Kurdish women in Turkey.[159] In combination with the state's "hands-off" approach to violence against women within Kurdish society for the sake of appeasing dissidence, in modern Turkey, Kurdish women have suffered doubly.

---

157. Kurdish Human Rights Project (London), "The Increase in Kurdish Women Committing Suicide," pp. 71–72.

158. KHRP, "Trial Observation Report, Turkey's Shame," p. 26.

159. Yüksel, "The Encounter of Kurdish Women," p. 777.

Chapter 5

The Kurdish Awakening:
Women Included

In the past three and a half decades, despite the Turkish state's efforts to either assimilate Kurds or to isolate them in benign ethnic enclaves, an increasingly articulate national Kurdish movement has arisen. It took root in the late 1960s, when, influenced by the spirit of worldwide socio-political revolutions and leftist-radical movements, domestic political unrest in Turkey, and the "upsurge of Kurdish nationalism in Iraq, led by younger Kurdish intelligentsia both in Kurdistan and in Istanbul, Ankara and other Turkish cities,"[160] Kurds started to organize against the Turkish establishment. After decades of relative inaction, disadvantage, abuse, and degradation, Kurdish women were a crucial part of this movement from its inception.

Starting in 1966, Kurdish youth in the Turkish capital of Ankara initiated a quiet but defiant movement. They smoked "Bitlis" cigarettes (the Kurdish name for the city where they were manufactured), attended mass meetings for democratic rights, and protested oppression.[161] At this time, Abdullah Öcalan, the future founder and leader of the Kurdistan Worker's Party (Partiye Karkerên Kurdistan — PKK), the longest-standing Kurdish nationalist organization to date (in Turkey) was living in Ankara, where the political activities transpiring around him awakened his political consciousness. In 1978, after a decade of repeated prison terms and having joined and left various Kurdish associations, Öcalan and a small group of university dropouts, young Kurdish men and women alike, gathered to plan a campaign for an independent Kurdish state under the auspices of the PKK.[162]

In the late 1970s, the founding PKK members and other contemporary dissident groups took advantage of the leeway provided by the economic and political crisis wreaking havoc throughout Turkey. Unlike most Kurdish organizations established in the 1970s, however, the PKK survived the 1980 military takeover of the government and its brutal campaigns to suppress opposition.[163] In fact, the repressive political climate instated by the leaders of

---

160. Hassanpour, "The Kurdish Experience," p. 7.

161. Marcus, *Blood and Belief*, p. 7.

162. Ibid., p. 1.

163. Hassanpour, "The Kurdish Experience," p. 7.

the coup only served to ignite the rage of the PKK members, and furthered their resolve to carry out their mission to establish an independent Kurdish state.

The Rise of the PKK: the Need to Mobilize Kurdish Women

Under Öcalan's directive, in 1984 the PKK successfully launched an armed uprising against the Turkish government and forces.[164] Although the initial clash between the PKK and the Turkish authorities seemed to benefit the PKK, Öcalan realized early on that sustaining his movement would require stronger backing of the Kurdish people. In order to acquire this backing, he needed to create a coalition from the disjointed Kurds of Turkey who were divided by strong tribal loyalties and the effects of Turkish policy, the two main obstacles to Kurdish cohesion. For Öcalan, the untapped resource of Kurdish women presented the most effective means by which he would attempt to unify his people.

According to Ceng Sagnic, a Kurdish rights activist and scholar, Öcalan's success hinged upon making traditional Kurdish opposition factions obsolete. Initially, Öcalan focused on overpowering the Kurdistan Democratic Party-Turkey (KDP-Turkey). Sagnic, who is grandson of Feqî Huseyn Sagnic, one of the founding members of the KDP-Turkey, contends that the PKK's principal rival was steeped in the tribal organization and customs of the Kurds. The greatest symbol of this system, Sagnic claims, were women, as "control of women is a fundamental aspect of tribal society." Öcalan recognized this axiom and knew that in order to upend the traditional Kurdish nationalists, who viewed themselves as the legitimate "engines of Kurdish nationalism," he would have to focus on the status of women. Öcalan suspected that if he could reshape the position of women in Kurdish society, he would be able to undermine the entire tribal system, which he saw as the main impediment to his leading the Kurdish liberation movement.[165] Altering the role of women, who were at the bottom of the tribal Kurdish hierarchy, he determined, was the best way to undermine tribal loyalty, to replace the tribe with the party, and to substitute the tribal leader for the party leader, that is, Öcalan.[166]

Indeed, at its start, the PKK recruited women as a tactic in its strategy to oust the traditional power holders of Kurdish society in Turkey and to replace them with PKK leaders. To facilitate this plan, Öcalan formulated a synthesized,

---

164. Marcus, *Blood and Belief*, p. 52.

165. Ceng Sagnic, Personal Interview, 20 February 2012.

166. Nihat Ali Özcan, "PKK Recruitment of Female Operatives," *Terrorism Focus*, Vol. 4, Issue 28, September 11, 2007, accessed August 27, 2011.

PKK-Marxist ideology prescribing an egalitarian view of women based on principles of gender equality in order to overcome the Kurdish social practice of gender discrimination. Although Öcalan managed to propagate an ideological framework through which he could implement these ideas, between 1978 and 1990, he faced a recruitment crisis due to the fact that most Kurds, men and women, still preferred to rely on the security provided by their tribes and families. According to the PKK's English website: "...in the first years of the PKK there were not many women throughout the organization..."[167] To circumvent this obstacle, the PKK allegedly drafted young women by kidnapping them.[168]

According to David Romano's research, reports of PKK units kidnapping youth, aged 16 to 25 (male and female), appeared in Turkish news sources in the late 1980s.[169] For the Kurds, this tactic may have "forced [hesitant] families whose children were already a member of the organization to cooperate," as well as encouraged young women to join as word spread that "women in the organization were 'free'."[170] Similar to bride kidnapping, it would be difficult to get a daughter back after she had been "kidnapped" by, or "eloped" with the PKK. Conversely, it is also possible that the term "kidnapped" was employed and circulated by the PKK in order to avoid reprisals by Turkish authorities against Kurdish communities suspected of colluding with the PKK.[171] If Turkish retaliation against Kurds for voluntarily joining the PKK made their lives more difficult than it was under their tribal leaders, Öcalan's recruitment challenges would have been further exacerbated, and counterproductive.

Sagnic adds, as the PKK originated in the context of Kemalist Turkey, it is possible to see this influence with regard to women and that "Öcalan... did [for Kurdish women] what Atatürk did for [Turkish] women."[172] From the beginning, the PKK allowed women to undertake non-traditional activities such as combat and non-combatant military functions and to serve as party journalists.[173] They were also taught to read, asked to participate in philosophical debates, and to write about the experience of being a Kurd and what it meant to

---

167. Delal Afsin Nurhak, "The Kurdistan Woman's Liberation Movement," Partiya Karkerên Kurdistan (PKK), accessed May 24, 2014.

168. Margaret Gonzalez-Perez, *Women and Terrorism: Female activity in domestic and international terror groups* (New York: Routledge, 2008), p. 87.

169. David Romano, *The Kurdish Nationalist Movement: Opportunity, Mobilization, and Identity* (Cambridge: Cambridge University Press, 2006), p. 77.

170. Nihat Ali Özcan, "PKK Recruitment of Female Operatives."

171. Romano, *The Kurdish Nationalist Movement*, p. 78.

172. Ceng Sagnic, Personal Interview, 22 February 2012.

173. Shahrzad Mojab, "Women and Nationalism in the Kurdish Republic of1946," in Shahrzad Mojab (ed.), *Women of a Non-State Nation: The Kurds* (Costa Mesa, CA: Mazda Publishers, Inc., 2001), p. 87.

them — opportunities most Kurdish women never received, either in village or urban settings.[174] As the PKK prohibits marriage and sexual relations, Kurdish women sidestepped the typical path of marriage and motherhood by joining. Furthermore, by forbidding marriage and sexual relations, PKK membership provided sanctuary from the *namus* code and thus offered Kurdish women lifestyle options (within a specific context) they otherwise would not have been able to pursue. In increasing numbers, Kurdish women — from villages, cities, and even from the Diaspora — gradually started to present themselves for service of their own volition.

Once recruitment of Kurdish women became more common (late 1980s and early 1990s), journalists and scholars of the Kurdish issue began to investigate the reasons these women elected to take up arms. In an interview conducted by journalist and filmmaker Kevin McKiernan, one female PKK member who rejected the inferior status of women in Kurdish society cited practices such as subjecting women to virginity tests before marriage, honor killings on suspicion of having had premarital sex, and the desire to escape such humiliation and danger as factors that strongly influenced many women's decision to join the PKK.[175] In Kurdish writer and poet Bejan Matur's book, *Dağın Ardına Bakmak (Looking Beyond the Mountain)*, interviews of former PKK male and female militants reveal that, for recruits, joining the PKK represented the only recourse they possessed to challenge "unjust Turkish state policies banning Kurdish culture, primarily embodied in Kurdish language." By joining the PKK, militants "heal and try to prevent the continuation of trauma" incurred from "political violence, poverty, dissatisfaction with immigration, and the loss of relatives in clashes with Turkish security forces."[176] For these PKK women, in exchange for their support against the Turkish authorities, they were promised equality and assured that if they fought for their freedom with their "own hands in the war, no one can take it away".[177] Consequently, less than a decade after the PKK launched its militant, pro-Kurdish campaign and effectively politicized the peasantry, unprecedented numbers of women were included in the national struggle for the first time in Kurdish history.[178] Yet, just as there were limitations

---

174. Ceng Sagnic, Personal Interview, 22 February 2012.
175. Kevin McKiernan, *The Kurds: A People in Search of Their Homeland* (New York: St. Martin's Press, 2006), p. 143.
176. Rasim Özgur Dönmez, "Book Review: *Dağın Ardına Bakmak (Looking Beyond the Mountain),*" *Ethnopolitics*, Vol. 11, Issue 1 (March 2012), pp. 117–119.
177. McKiernan, *The Kurds*, pp. 158–159.
178. Anna Secor, "'There is an Istanbul That Belongs to Me': Citizenship, Space and Identity in the City," *Annals of the Association of American Geographers*, Vol. 94, No. 2 (June 2004), p. 356.

within the Turkish women's liberation movement under Kemalism, so too were there in the Kurdish women's liberation movement under the PKK.

The Limitations of PKK Rhetoric: Defining the Scope and Meaning of Kurdish Women's Empowerment within the Ranks of the PKK

Although Öcalan touted the PKK as the Movement of Women's Emancipation,[179] and continues to call for the double liberation of Kurdish men and women as "the rebirth of free woman will inevitably result in general emancipation, enlightenment and justice,"[180] inconsistencies between rhetoric and reality in the organization persist. Although the PKK espouses a particular ideology of equality, gender rights, and an end to feudal and tribal practices for both female and male recruits, early membership did not translate into the immediate rejection of the patriarchal culture and the customs such social systems foster. Notably, however, the early shortcomings in the actualization of Öcalan's gender equality teachings provide a way to identify the time period in which, born out of the national struggle, a women's rights consciousness appeared.

In the mid to late 1980s, gender equality consciousness was not widespread among Kurdish men and women in Turkey. An event that supports this claim took place in 1987, when "women fighters in the ranks of the PKK established YJWK."[181] Founded in Hannover, Germany, the platform of the Yêkitîya Jinên Welatparêzên Kurdistanê (the Union of the Patriotic Women of Kurdistan)[182] stated that all forms of violence and oppression faced by Kurdish women resulted from the Turkish occupation of Kurdistan.[183] As such, according to human rights lawyer and researcher, Susan McDonald, the YJWK advocated, first and foremost, a free Kurdistan, after which women's liberation would be

179. Ali Kemal Özcan, *Turkey's Kurds*, p. 170.

180. "Patriarchy — the Enslavement of Women," from "All Articles" on the Partiya Karkaren Kurdistan (PKK) Website in English, accessed August 21, 2011.

181. Nurhak, "The Kurdistan Woman's Liberation Movement," Partiya Karkerên Kurdistan (PKK).

182. Koma Jinên Bilind, "The Kurdistan Women's Liberation Movement for a Universal Women's Struggle," The High Women's Council — KJB (Koma Jinên Bilind), March 2011, accessed May 26, 2014.

183. Nazand Bagikhani, "Kurdish Women and National Identity," *KurdishMedia.com*, November 8, 2003, accessed April 30, 2011.

pursued.[184] According to McDonald's research, the YJWK prioritized national liberation over women's liberation and attributed the inferior status of women to the Turkish occupation rather than internal Kurd-supported discriminatory gender structures. In contrast, Delal Afsin Nurhak, a female-PKK member writing for the organization's official English website, claims that the decision to form the YJWK came from recognizing the "feudal characteristics of Kurdish society of the time," which made it "understandable why Kurdish women decided to organize independently in order to better fulfill their role in the liberation movement."[185]

From these two somewhat contradictory points of view, it is at least possible to identify a tension between PKK policy and practice vis-à-vis women. Kurdish women had joined the PKK to escape gender constraints and create a new reality for themselves, yet Öcalan's call for the reexamination and reformation of gender roles within Kurdish society for the purpose of securing women's rights and Kurdish liberation from the yoke of the Turkish state's repression had yet to be fully internalized and practiced.

In the early days of the insurgency this gap was apparent: female militants carried out military operations together with their male counterparts until the number of sexual harassment incidents forced a separation of units by gender.[186] In the same time period, women were precluded from holding top leadership positions.[187] Presumably, then, female PKK fighters dissatisfied with the shortcomings of their organization formed the YJWK. However, a women's liberation agenda within the PKK, at that point, had yet to be fully articulated.

Closing the Gap: PKK Women Pursue the Meaning and Dimensions of Gender Parity

According to gender scholar Nira Yuval-Davis, it is common for an organization fighting for a nationalist cause that employs gender discourse in pursuit of its goals to perpetuate a divergence between that discourse and actual gender relations.[188] In the case of the PKK, initially, Yuval-Davis' theory held true. However, the rhetoric of prioritizing the nation's rights over women's did

---

184. McDonald, "Kurdish Women and Self-Determination: A Feminist Approach to International Law," p. 150.
185. Nurhak, "The Kurdistan Woman's Liberation Movement," Partiya Karkerên Kurdistan (PKK).
186. Nihat Ali Özcan, "PKK Recruitment of Female Operatives."
187. Mojab, "Women and Nationalism in the Kurdish Republic of 1946," p. 87.
188. Yuval-Davis, Gender and Nation, p. 39.

not impede the formulation of a women's rights consciousness among PKK women for long. Rather, according to Metin Yüksel, the militarization and the popularization of Kurdish nationalism in the 1980s and 1990s (primarily facilitated by the PKK) led to the development of "a womanhood and/or feminist consciousness" that began to question the prevalent sexism of Kurdish society and the limitations it placed on them.[189] As an example, women such as Commander Rengin (name given in article), who joined the PKK in 1990 at the age of 14 in order to fight for Kurdish rights, elected to "go to war" because "women grow up enslaved by society. The minute you are born as a girl, society inhibits you . . . If I am a woman, I need to be known by the strength of my womanhood, to get respect. Those are my rights," she claimed.[190]

Another early incidence of this newfound agency is clearly illustrated by the story of Kesire Yıldırım, PKK founder Öcalan's ex-wife, a PKK co-founder, and member of the party. Interestingly, Yıldırım was an Alevi Kurd and it was believed that Öcalan chose to marry her so as to fortify an alliance between the Alevi and Sunni Kurds. She received the code name "Fatma," and Öcalan became "Ali."[191] Yıldırım was a member of the PKK Politburo until 1988. Although the details of the incident are unclear, in the late 1980s Yıldırım sought to remove her husband from his position as chairman of the Politburo and lead in his stead. Following her failed attempt, she fled to Europe with her fellow dissidents where she tried to establish an alternative PKK Politburo. Although the idea of a politically prominent woman in Kurdish society is not an historical anomaly, Martin van Bruinessen uses this case to illustrate that, even though she failed, Yıldırım's attempt "showed that the idea of a woman becoming a political leader through her own strength" had become conceivable in contemporary Kurdish society.[192]

Moreover, the mere circumstances of a rapidly escalating insurgency forced the PKK to put female recruits into leadership positions relatively quickly. To illustrate this point, at the level of the day-to-day insurgency in 1987, only one percent of PKK fighters were female.[193] By 1993, the first women-only guerilla

---

189. Yüksel, "The Encounter of Kurdish Women with Nationalism in Turkey," p. 780.

190. Arwa Damon, "Female Fighters: We won't stand for male dominance," *Cnn.com International*, October 6, 2008, accessed August 24, 2011.

191. Dünya Başol, "The Impact of Religion on Kurdish Nationalism," a public lecture delivered to the Forum on Kurdish Society, History and Culture of the Moshe Dayan Center for Middle Eastern and African Studies, T el Aviv University, Tel Aviv, Israel, April 2, 2012.

192. van Bruinessen, "From Adela Khanum to Leyla Zana," p. 106.

193. Dryaz, "Women and Nationalism: How Women Activists are Changing the Kurdish Conflict."

units were formed, leading to the establishment of a "women's army," which also carried out social and political activities in Kurdish villages and cities.[194] In the late 1990s, 30 percent of the PKK's 17,000 armed militant recruits were women. Some of these women rose to the rank of "commando," and the majority claimed equal participation in the Party's rank and file.[195] As of 2007, the PKK's armed wing for self-defense had a 40 percent mandatory quota for female commanders.[196]

As the realization that women could and did contribute as much as men to the movement within the PKK, an organized women's liberation movement speedily materialized outside the realm of militant action against the Turkish state. In 1995, the first Kurdistan Women's Liberation Congress convened under the Kurdistan Free Women's Union (YAJK — Yekîtiya Azadiya Jinên Kurdistanê), which brought together Kurdish women who had fought as PKK militants. Members of YAJK claimed the experience as fighters helped them "to develop their own social and political perspective instead of copying male-like characteristics or assuming themselves as a back-up force." Touting itself as part of the international women's movement, the YAJK even participated in the 1995 UN Women's Conference in Beijing.[197]

On March 8, 1999, the Kurdistan Working Women's Party (PJKK) was established.[198] This organization gave itself the mandate to create a practical and tangible approach to the March 8, 1998, "Women's Liberation Ideology," a directive announced by Öcalan "to integrate the struggle of women of Kurdistan with the struggle of the women of the world" and aimed "to reorganize the whole of society by renovating the matriarchal order of life that existed in natural societies."[199] In fact, Öcalan continued to emphasize the gender equality aspect of the Kurdish struggle even from his prison cell when, in 1999, he called upon "ancient history" to justify the need for Kurdish society to break with patriarchal customs, and claimed that doing so would be a return to authentic, Kurdish ancestral tradition.[200]

---

194. Koma Jinên Bilind, "The Kurdistan Women's Liberation Movement for a Universal Women's Struggle."

195. McDonald, "Kurdish Women and Self-Determination," p. 148; Nihat Ali Oczan, "PKK Recruitment of Female Operatives."

196. Deborah Haynes, "The Kurdish Women Rebels Who are Ready to Fight and Die for the Kurdish Cause," *KurdNet*, October 24, 2007, accessed August 28, 2011.

197. Koma Jinên Bilind, "The Kurdistan Women's Liberation Movement for a Universal Women's Struggle."

198. Ibid.

199. Nurhak, "The Kurdistan Woman's Liberation Movement," Partiya Karkerên Kurdistan (PKK).

200. International Free Movement's Foundation, *Psychological Consequences*, p. 22.

PKK women-led initiatives to achieve Öcalan's vision of women's liberation enjoined and still include several successor parties and events. For example, in 2000, the PJKK morphed into the Partiya Jina Azad, the Women's Liberation Party, which hosted conferences and activities to "strengthen the cooperation and dialogues with women from all over the world."[201] Under the auspices of the PKK, these organizations have sought to influence broader Kurdish society as well. For instance, in 2003, the PKK issued an edict reflecting the ideology and approach of women's organizations, stating, "All laws reflecting male domination should be annulled. Violence against all women, all forms of control on women's bodies and lives resulting from outdated custom and traditional habits, and bride prices should be forbidden."[202] The PKK's dissemination of such a proclamation encouraged Kurdish men to join the Kurdish women's rights struggle, too.

In 2004, the Kurdistan Women's Liberation Party (Partiya Azadiya Jin a Kurdistan — "The Women's Ideological Movement") came into being and sought to serve as an inclusive Kurdish women's organization to promote women's liberation.[203] A currently active PKK women's organization is the High Women's Council (KJB — Koma Jinên Bilind), established in 2005 and operating both at the local and international level. The KJB promotes the historical viewpoint, as expressed by Öcalan in his writings from 2006 that women used to be revered and worshiped for their ability to give birth as well as for agricultural skills. However, a "gender conflict" arose between 2000-1700 B.C.E., when Sumerian mythology chronicles friction between male gods and powerful "creative goddesses" that were eventually marginalized. This period, according to Öcalan, marks the transition from matriarchal social organization to a patriarchal one. As the Kurds were contemporaries and subscribers to the Sumerian system of law and order, Öcalan argues, one of the PKK's tasks is to restore the historic, revered legacy of women in Kurdish society.[204]

To the present day, the KJB coordinates PKK sponsored programs that offer coaching on the rights of women, a "practical unit" that addresses problems of inequality, and a section that oversees the female military role in the PKK.[205] In order to carry out this mission, the KJB educates men and women on gender rights by teaching a required course for PKK fighters called "Kill the man in

201. Koma Jinên Bilind, "The Kurdistan Women's Liberation Movement for a Universal Women's Struggle."
202. Argue, "Kurdish Culture, Repression, Women's Rights, and Resistance."
203. Koma Jinên Bilind, "The Kurdistan Women's Liberation Movement for a Universal Women's Struggle."
204. International Free Movement's Foundation, *Psychological Consequences*, p. 22.
205. Haynes, "The Kurdish Women Rebels…"

you." These kinds of programs continue to attract Kurdish women both inside and out of Turkey.[206] Moreover, they illustrate Kurdish women's internalization and integration of Öcalan's rhetoric on the liberation of women, and how women are now carrying out concrete measures to change their day-to-day reality.

The continued voluntary enlistment of Kurdish women in the PKK is a testament to the success of its efforts to brand itself as the Kurdish women's emancipation movement. So too are the active factions of PKK women's organizations (established in 2005), which include the Free Women's Union (Yektiyên Jinên Azad — "The Women's Social Unit"), the Free Women's Union-Star (Yektiyên Jinên Azad Star — YJA Star — "The Women's Self-Defense Force"),[207] and the Committee of Young Women (a subsection of the KJB).[208]

The PKK continues to attract Kurdish women from all socioeconomic sectors — from rural areas, urban centers, universities, and also from the Kurdish Diaspora of Europe.[209] In June 2011, the Turkish daily newspaper *Hürriyet* reported on the publication of the first academic study on the PKK conducted by a Turkish organization. From a sample of over 400 individuals analyzed by the Ankara-based Economy Policy Research Foundation of Turkey, most female PKK members come from the southeastern cities of Hakkari and Mardin, followed by Diyarbakır, Bitlis, and Van. Particularly in Hakkari, where low enrollment of girls in schools and forced marriages of teenage girls are prevalent, recruitment numbers are the highest. Istanbul alone accounts for 20 percent of new members, making it the highest of all urban centers where the PKK seeks out recruits.[210]

Over the past decade, volunteers from Iraqi Kurdistan have also joined the PKK. Often, these are Kurdish women escaping honor killings. They either elect or are sent by their families to seek refuge by joining the PKK, whose operative cells are mainly in the Qandil Mountains of Northern Iraq.[211] Not only are these women's lives saved, but they are also instilled with the PKK's brand of feminism. Similarly, in pursuit of alternatives to the lives their communities

---

206. Boris Kalnoky, "Feminists and terrorists? Women and the PKK," *Women in Focus*, April 14, 2010, accessed August 28, 2011.

207. Nurhak, "The Kurdistan Woman's Liberation Movement," Partiya Karkerên Kurdistan (PKK).

208. Koma Jinên Bilind, "The Kurdistan Women's Liberation Movement for a Universal Women's Struggle."

209. Nihat Ali Özcan, "PKK Recruitment of Female Operatives."

210. *Hürriyet Daily News*, "First Academic Research on PKK's Demographics," *Hürriyet Daily News*, July 18, 2011, accessed August 2, 2011.

211. Kalnoky, "Feminists and Terrorists? Women and the PKK."

expect them to lead, and in order to flee retaliation for breaching the *namus* code of traditional Kurdish society, Kurdish women from Syria and Iran are also joining the ranks of the PKK.[212] Of course, Kurdish women continue to join the PKK in pursuit of realizing Kurdish ethno-national aspirations as well.

The Boundaries of PKK Feminism/Women's Rights

Öcalan intended for the PKK to crystallize as a mass Kurdish resistance movement that would galvanize the Kurdish population in support of a unified nationalist cause that eschewed traditional, conservative, patriarchal customs, embodied by the liberation of Kurdish women from a shackled past. It is important to mention, however, the limitations of the PKK's influence on the advancement of Kurdish women in Turkey. Despite PKK women's progress and their ongoing women's liberation-focused activities, the PKK continues to fall short of many of its women's rights aspirations.

Inarguably, the PKK created an infrastructure for education, leadership, military, and semi-professional training for women. As previously mentioned, the results of these efforts include empowerment, a sense of agency, and a refuge from Kurdish society's expectations of women. However, for ideological reasons and despite the claims of being part of an international women's rights struggle, the PKK does not necessarily have the capability to promote this framework beyond its ranks and activities in greater Kurdish communities. For example, according to Ceng Sagnic, the towns and villages along the Turkish-Iraqi border are often visited by PKK troops in the four months of winter when inclement weather inhibits the patrol of Turkish forces. These are often the months during which the PKK declares unilateral ceasefires because it is too difficult to stage attacks in such harsh weather conditions.[213] In those months, the PKK restocks its supplies and uses its finely tuned propaganda machine to seek out new recruits to replace those who have perished or left the group. While the PKK does not force Kurdish youngsters to join its ranks, it does encourage young men and women to come and study with them in the nearby mountains, where the PKK has its classrooms in caves and makeshift structures. As a PKK "friend," it is possible to learn to read and write, and to make new friends. PKK women focus on other young women, tell them about the freedom they possess, and show

---

212. Paul Schemm, "Kurdish Fighters Offer Guerilla Feminism," *AFP*, November 28, 2006, found on: *Kurdish Aspect — Kurdish News and Points of View*, accessed August 28, 2011.

213. *Today's Zaman*, "PKK Ceasefire End Seen as Move to Help BDP Before Elections" *Today's Zaman*, March 2, 2011, accessed March 1, 2012.

them the camaraderie they enjoy with their cohorts. As young women in these communities have almost no opportunity for a life outside the village, "the PKK offers the world," says Sagnic. However, encouragement to learn and grow is contingent upon joining the PKK. To that effect, the organization does not use its propaganda campaigns to encourage Kurdish parents to send their girls to Turkish schools, as they are run by the state and thus, for the PKK, tainted by the "Turkish capitalist system."[214]

Originally, the PKK envisioned its role in the Kurdish national movement as the liberators of the Kurds and Kurdish women as well. This idea is clear from the recordings of PKK Congress meetings in the 1990s, wherein quasi-state building measures were introduced, such as commitment to build economic, cultural, health, and academic institutions. Regarding women, reportedly, at the Fifth Congress of the PKK held in 1995, the organization reaffirmed its mission to end all forms of oppression against women, to realize the equal status of men and women in Kurdish society in all areas of social and political life, and vowed to promote women possessing "an enormous revolutionary dynamic" to prominent positions of leadership.[215] Nevertheless, with the capture of Öcalan in 1999, followed by a decade of waffling between a call for full sovereignty to true citizenship within Turkey for the Kurds, the PKK has demonstrated the limits of its influence. For example, in 2002, in accordance with Öcalan's orders, thousands of fighters laid down their arms in a temporary ceasefire. PKK women who did so discovered that once they left the ranks of the organization where they were, literally, equal with men, the return to Kurdish society revealed the disconnect between the PKK's world and the realities most Kurdish women continue to face.

During the periodic, short-lived ceasefires that occurred in the first decade of the twenty-first century, thousands of PKK fighters resigned from the organization at the urging of an imprisoned Öcalan[216] as a gesture of good will to the Turkish authorities. Many resettled in Iraqi Kurdistan where they received Iraqi citizenship, whereas others surrendered to Turkey in hopes of eventually becoming politically involved or simply returning home. In 2004, while attending the University of Duhok in Iraqi Kurdistan, Sagnic became acquainted with a distant cousin, an ex-PKK fighter by the name of Çîmen. Çîmen had been an important and highly respected PKK commander who

---

214. Ceng Sagnic, Personal Interview, 22 February 2012.

215. "The Revolution in Kurdistan, 5th Congress, Kurdistan Workers Party (PKK), 24 January 1995: PKK Party Program, Chapter Three," translated by *Arm the Spirit, For A Free And Independent Kurdistan! KURD-L Archives*, accessed January 22, 2011.

216. Selcuk Kapuçi, "PKK members: Ergenekon prevented our release," *Today's Zaman*, October 21, 2009, accessed January 10, 2012.

resigned and married a fellow ex-guerrilla who had lost his legs in combat. When Sagnic met her, Çîmen and her husband were living in a shared house where former PKK fighters stay until they manage to secure jobs and become financially stable enough to rent their own homes. Çîmen's husband turned out to be abusive and an alcoholic. Eventually, she divorced him. She now lives alone and supports herself. Sagnic claims Çîmen's case is one of many, although not every former-PKK female fighter has the courage to pursue divorce from an abusive husband or unsatisfying marriage. After ten to fifteen years of fighting, many former PKK female guerrillas have ended up forming traditional families, and have ultimately resumed the lifestyles they thought they had escaped.[217]

Conversely, there are cases of former PKK female militants who have become active, influential players in the national movement from within Turkey through formal politics and journalism. For example, Yüksel Genç surrendered to the Turkish authorities in 1999 among many others who did so in the same year as a symbolic gesture of peace.[218] After serving a prison term for her involvement in the PKK, Genç continued to utilize the professional and leadership skills she acquired in the PKK. She became an advocate for Kurdish rights via the EU Turkey Civic Commission, where in 2010 she charged the currently ruling Justice and Development Party (AKP) with trying to combat Kurdish nationalism by portraying Kurds and Turks as "Muslim brethren," which undermined the fact that while Kurds want equality with Turks, they still want their differences to be recognized. In 2011, she became the editor of *Özgür Gündem (Free Agenda)*, a controversial independent Turkish newspaper that, at times, has been the only media source in Turkey that reports on the activities of the PKK and the Kurdish struggle.[219] Through *Özgür Gündem*, she has harshly criticized the AKP's handling of the Kurdish issue. In 2011, the authorities implicated Genç in committing acts of sedition for her outspokenness against the state.[220] She was detained with 49 other journalists on December 20, 2011, and put in the Bakırköy Prison for Women and Juveniles for alleged association with the Kurdish Communities Union (KCK), identified by the Turkish state as

---

217. Ceng Sagnic, Personal Interview, February, 22, 2012.

218. Kapuçi, "PKK Members: Ergenekon Prevented Our Release."

219. Committee to Protect Journalists, "Ocak Isik Yurtcu, Former Editor in Chief, Ozgur Gundem, Turkey, Currently Serving a 15-year Prison Sentence for Disseminating 'Separatist Propaganda'," Committee to Protect Journalists, accessed August 3, 2012.

220. Wladimir van Wilgenburg, "PKK and Islamic Gulen Movement Clash in Turkey," *Rudaw.net*, December 18, 2010, accessed November 5, 2011.

an urban arm of the PKK. [221] Incarcerated on December 24, 2011, Yüksel Genç remained in prison without a conviction[222] for 29 months.[223]

Measuring the PKK's Success on Its Women Agenda

Despite its shortcomings, ultimately, the PKK succeeded in creating a legitimate and socially acceptable alternative to marriage and to the traditional, subservient role apportioned to women in Kurdish society.[224] Moreover, by the end of the twentieth century it became clear that the PKK had initiated the first large-scale grassroots movement in Kurdish history, and this was only possible due to the participation of women from all walks of Kurdish society. Although the influence of the PKK on the notion of independent women fully participating in Kurdish society is limited by the PKK itself, Kurdish women, en masse, have witnessed what they can accomplish when given the necessary resources. For Kurdish women in Turkey, the PKK, through its inclusion of women in the articulation and implementation of the national movement, and the roles women fulfill in the organization and its objectives, has inaugurated nothing less than a revolution in the perception and role of the common Kurdish woman. Despite the shortcomings, the neoteric notion of empowered women has managed to transcend the boundaries of the PKK, its operations, and its operatives.

Both women who are members and women who are not affiliated with the PKK vouch for the vital role it has played in triggering a demand for national rights as well as women's rights. According to testimony given by an active female PKK member in 2003, her political involvement conferred upon her confidence and pride in her identity. It provided a context in which, she claimed, a Kurdish woman could become an active agent in her own history making.[225] Similarly, based upon her research in Istanbul among members of displaced Kurdish communities, and particularly of women, Anna Secor found that "women frequently attributed their own active self-positioning as Kurds to

221. Yüksel Genç, "Who is Deceiving Whom?," *ANF News Agency*, January 23, 2012, accessed February 5, 2012.

222. European Federation of Journalists, "Latest News in Set Journalists Free in Turkey Campaign — Archive," European Federation of Journalists, March 10, 2013, accessed March 10, 2013.

223. Elif Akgül, "29 Ay Sonra Gelen Serbestliği Konşutular," *Bianet*, May 13, 2014, accessed January 7, 2015.

224. van Bruinessen, "From Adela Khanum to Leyla Zana," pp. 105–106.

225. Nazand Bagikhani, "Kurdish Women and National Identity," *KurdishMedia.com*, November 8, 2003, accessed April 30, 2011.

changes in Turkish society since the early 1980s," and cited one Kurdish woman who claimed that "the expression of Kurdish identity was more possible today than it was 20 years ago and ... those who did try to explain these changes pointed toward the effects of the PKK's armed uprising."[226]

226. Secor, "There is an Istanbul that Belongs to Me," p. 364. According to the author, for fear of accusation of being a terrorist or sympathizer with a terrorist group, some women hesitated to acknowledge the role of the PKK in this transformation.

"Halay" dances on the road from Istanbul to the Peace and Democracy Party's (BDP) Women's Congress in Ankara, April 28, 2013.

Photo by Eva Bernard

A Kurdish woman waves the Free Democratic Women's Movement flag (DÖKH), at the BDP Women's Congress in Ankara, April 29, 2013.

Photo by Eva Bernard

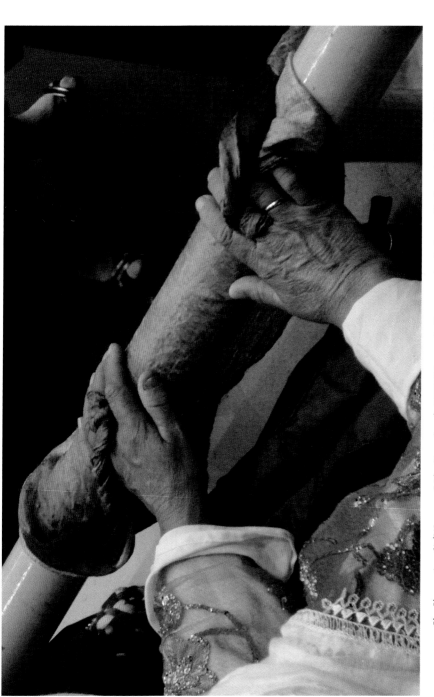

Jin Jiyan Azadî (Women, Life, Freedom), BDP Women's Congress in Ankara, Turkey, April 29, 2013.

Photo by Eva Bernard

Dilşa Deniz, Kurdish anthropologist and author, in Istanbul, Turkey, September 27, 2013.

Photo by Heidi Basch-Harod

Chapter 6

The Rise of Kurdish Women's Rights Consciousness in the Context of an Evolving Turkish State

Mojab and Gorman concur that the first political struggles for women's emancipation coincided with the rise of nations, nationalism, and the nation-state of the "bourgeois democratic revolutions of the eighteenth century."[227] Accordingly, Hassanpour and Mojab contend that the discussion on gender equality among the Kurds first emerged in the Kurdish press of the early twentieth century as part of the Ottoman-Kurdish nationalist discourse, and took its inspiration from the liberal feminist and women's movements of the late nineteenth and early twentieth centuries in Europe.[228] Having been postponed during the debilitating "silent decades," when discourse on the "woman question" all but disappeared among the Kurds, it is fair to infer that a natural outcome of the late twentieth century Kurdish national struggle would, once again, include a revisiting of the "woman question."

Certainly, the Kurdish national struggle and Turkey's handling of the Kurdish Question in the late twentieth century and the early twenty-first century deeply influenced, and still contributes to, the discussion of Kurdish women in Turkey and the evolution of a Kurdish women's rights consciousness. However, these represent only two of four factors that initially impacted and facilitated the awakening. The third factor was the Turkish women's rights movement, which evolved in its scope, approach, and agenda at the same time that the Kurdish national movement was re-emerging. Indeed, in the period under discussion, Kurdish women looked to, emulated, and sometimes joined in the activities of Turkish women in the pursuit of shared and individual goals. After all, they held in common a formidable opponent — the Turkish state. Regarding Turkey, the country began its ongoing accession process to the European Union (then called the European Community), which is the fourth factor that contributed to an environment in which a Kurdish women's movement began to flourish. With

227. Mojab and Gorman, "Dispersed Nationalism," p. 59.
228. Mojab and Hassanpour, "In Memory of Fadime Sahindal," p. 2.

Turkey under the scrutiny of the European Community, the process afforded new opportunities for both Kurds and women to pursue political platforms and to make demands that were previously difficult or impossible.

By the last decade of the twentieth century, the combination of these four factors contributed to the development of a unique and distinctly Kurdish women's rights movement, specifically representing and advocating on behalf of the particular situation of Kurdish women in Turkey. In its attempt to tackle the issues that perpetuate the double oppression of Kurdish women today, there are manifestations of this movement from the upper echelons of Kurdish women's political involvement to the grassroots level. Kurdish women's interactions (outside the PKK) with and against an evolving Turkish state (vis-à-vis the Kurdish question and the women's rights movement of Turkey as Turkey sought EU membership) contributed to the rise of a Kurdish women's rights consciousness and movement. The significance of this current state of affairs cannot be overstated and lends to a hopeful future for the Kurdish women of Turkey despite centuries-old challenges that refuse to disappear.

The Evolving Understanding of Women's Rights in the Republic of Turkey: A Focus on the "Individual" and Violence Against Women

Since 1923, the "woman question" in Turkey, primarily framed by men, dealt exclusively with issues concerning access to education, political enfranchisement, and dress.[229] Accordingly, Metin Yüksel argues, although Kemalism represented a progressive ideology that encouraged women's participation in society, particularly in education and professions, it did not challenge patriarchal norms of morality and thus merely replaced the "Islamic patriarchy" of the Ottoman Empire with "nation-state patriarchy."[230] Indeed, as late as 1994, Leyla Zana, the first Kurdish woman elected to the Turkish parliament, remarked that for both Kurdish and Turkish women in Turkey who did manage to overcome the gender barrier and rise to positions of public and political power, most were used as "token women" and held office merely by the will and permission of men.[231] Consequently, Jenny White claims, this top-

---

229. Anna Louie Sussman, "Why Turkey is Backsliding on Women's Rights," *The Atlantic*, June 16, 2011, accessed June 27, 2011. The similar ways in which the "woman question" in Kurdish nationalist circles excluded or used Kurdish women for a political agenda have been discussed in previous chapters.

230. Yüksel, "The Encounter of Kurdish Women with Nationalism in Turkey," p. 781.

231. Leyla Zana, *Writings from Prison*, p. 12.

down "state feminism" never empowered women as individuals and, further, the realm of the private sphere remained untouchable.[232]

In the 1980s, for the first time in the country's history, women's voices called for individual rights and individualism, and sought solutions to the shortcomings of those notions that they experienced as women in Turkey.[233] According to Deniz Kandiyoti, by the late 1980s this new generation of self-proclaimed feminists started to publicly address cultural taboos such as domestic violence, sexual harassment, and rape — the social ills not included on the state-approved list of women's issues.[234] Even "Kemalist feminists" began to challenge status quo when, in 1985, women from this political camp initiated a campaign to amend the Turkish Civil Code and its designation of the male/husband as the recognized head of the family.[235]

An examination of the Kemalist approach to women's rights revealed how the state precluded and discouraged discourse on the shaping of a women's movement that included discussion of religious and ethnic identity — the only type of movement, according to Yüksel, that could meaningfully influence the lives of Kurdish women and Turkish ones, too.[236] In the late 1980s, the monopoly of Kemalism on dictating the role of women and the dimensions of the "woman question" in Turkey began to wane, and the state-led approach to women's rights policy (whose true intent was the building of a cohesive and homogeneous national identity) also came under question. With this development, to a limited extent, Kurdish women began to enter the mainstream discourse of the Turkish women's rights movement. To be sure, the women's movement of the Kemalist-dominated era ignored Kurdishness and the plight of the Kurds (in many cases out of safety concerns vis-à-vis the state authorities). By the 1990s, however, Turkish women's rights activists, either in ideology or by action, sought alliances with Kurdish women's groups to address the shared conflict with the state and its policies against women and their interests.[237]

---

232. J.B. White, "State Feminism, Modernization, and the Turkish Republican Woman," *NWSA Journal*, Vol. 15, No. 3, *Gender and Modernism Between the Wars* (Autumn 2003), p. 157.

233. Yeşim Arat, "Democracy and Women in Turkey: In Defense of Liberalism," *Social Politics*, Vol. 6, No. 3 (Fall 1999), pp. 370–387.

234. Deniz Kandiyoti, "A Tangled Web: the Politics of Gender in Turkey," *Open Democracy*, January 5, 2011, accessed January 13, 2011.

235. Arat, "Democracy and Women in Turkey," p. 375.

236. Yüksel, "The Encounter of Kurdish Women," p. 782.

237. Kathryn Cameron Porter, "Disappearances — an Alarming Trend," *American Kurdish Information Network (AKIN)*, January 2, 1997, accessed August 22, 2012.

Fortifying the developing awareness and activism around a woman-led women's rights movement, in the late 1980s, Turkey submitted its application for formal membership to the European Community.[238] In order to become eligible to commence the accession process, though, Turkey was required to formulate and implement a number of policy reforms. Particularly, its poor human rights record on several issues including the status of women, sorely needed improvement.[239] Subsequently, the women's movement in Turkey began to benefit from the country being under the microscope of EC monitors.

In this atmosphere of possibility and reform, Kurdish and Turkish women's rights activists alike began to recognize that the struggle for gender equality was "part and parcel of the struggle for greater pluralism and an inclusive democracy in Turkey," the achievement of which would result in the recognition of the Kurdish people in some legitimate manner.[240] Of course, neither all Kurdish women nor all Turkish women's groups were willing or interested in collaborating with one another. With respect to the violent history of the past three decades between Kurds and Turks, to some extent this tension prevails to the present day. Despite their differences, however, in 1996 a contributor to a Kurdish women's journal, *Roza*, wrote "we learned a lot from Turkish women... how to perform an action by ourselves, to act with solidarity..."[241] Similarly, in 2001, in the Kurdish women's journal *Jin û Jiyan (Woman and Life)*, another woman wrote that they learned from Turkish feminists "that the private is political, ...and how the woman consciousness can be raised."[242]

The Double Struggle of Kurdish Women for National Recognition and Women's Rights

In a 1993 interview with Leyla Zana, she shared that "everywhere in the world women are ill-treated by men but amongst Kurds it is especially bad. A woman

238. Cameron Lyons, "Why the EU Needs Turkey: A Case for Accession," *Northeastern University Political Review* (February 3, 2011), accessed June 26, 2013. Turkey's application was submitted on April 14, 1987.
239. Graham E. Fuller, "The Fate of the Kurds," *Foreign Affairs*, Vol. 72, No. 2 (Spring 1993), p. 117.
240. Pinar Ilkkaracan, "The 'Turkish model': for whom?," *Open Democracy*, November 9, 2011, accessed December 2, 2011.
241. Ömer Çaha, "The Kurdish Women's Movement: A Third-Wave Feminism within the Kurdish Conext," *Turkish Studies*, Vol. 12, No. 3 (September 2011), p. 439.
242. Çaha, "The Kurdish Women's Movement," p. 439.

is not even treated as a servant, she is a thing, almost an animal."[243] On top of which, writing in the early 1990s, Graham E. Fuller, a senior political scientist of the RAND Corporation, noted that of the four countries that the majority of Kurds inhabit, Turkey has practiced the most repressive cultural policy toward the Kurds.[244] As previously discussed, the manifestations of this policy include the prohibition of the use of Kurdish language, the codification of severe punitive measures for any other expression of Kurdishness, population transfers, and state-sanctioned, extrajudicial violence against Kurdish civilians suspected of sympathizing with the PKK. In the late twentieth century, then, to be a Kurdish woman in Turkey inherently foretold a destiny of hardship, discrimination, violence, and intimidation. Yet, out of the experience of the double plight endured by Kurdish women (as Kurds in an ethnocentric state and as females), as women existing in two male-dominated societies, both Turkish and Kurdish, the distinctive Kurdish women's movement became dual-faceted as well. The following paragraphs outline the events and factors that contributed to this process, which include Turkey's dealing with the Kurdish question, Kurdish reactions to these efforts, and developments in the women's rights movement of Turkey, all in the context of Turkey's desire to join the European Union.

In the 1980s, Turkey responded to the re-invigorated Kurdish national movement by strictly enforcing the 1982 constitution. This document declared Turkish as the mother tongue of all citizens of Turkey, made mentioning the words "Kurd" and "Kurdistan" grounds for treason, and outlined emergency-rule laws that granted the military "free rein" in the southeast of Turkey from where the majority of PKK members originated.[245] Between 1989 and 2000, according to the İnsan Hakları Derneği (İHD — Human Rights Association; a Turkish NGO founded in 1986), 1,964 persons (80 percent from the Kurdish region) "'disappeared' as a result of 'killings by unknown perpetrators,'" and 3,438 settlements in rural areas were evacuated, leading to the forced migration of approximately 4 to 4.5 million citizens of Turkey, whose mother tongue was Kurdish.[246] Notably, there is a dispute over the accurate number of internally displaced Kurds in Turkey. The Turkish Ministry of the Interior counts less than 400,000 internally displaced persons. However, the Kurdish Human Rights Project and the Bar Human Rights Committee of England and Wales claim that this figure includes only "persons displaced as a result of village and hamlet evacuations in the south-east [sic], and does not include people who fled

---

243. Chris Kutschera, "A Silent Scream," *The Middle East*, No. 27, (October 1993), pp. 33.
244. Fuller, "The Fate of the Kurds," p. 111.
245. Watts, "Pro-Kurdish Parties," p. 635.
246. International Free Women's Foundation, *Psychological Trauma*, p. 34.

violence stemming from the conflict between the government and the Kurdistan Workers' Party (PKK), which included evacuations, spontaneous movement, displacement and related rural to urban movement within the south-east itself."[247]

As in the decades following World War I, aware of the gravity that rape and sexual violence bears in traditional and patriarchal societies such as that of the Kurds, Turkey intentionally targeted women in order to destabilize, delegitimize, and deter Kurds from participating in the PKK's struggle against the state, and to turn the Kurds against the PKK.[248] The effects of these tactics were manifold and are still felt today. For Kurdish women, the ongoing repercussions of the combination of state-sanctioned practices include impoverishment, social and psychological damages, and severe mistrust of the state and its representatives due to the abductions, detentions, and sexual and psychological torture often carried out by plainclothes members of the police or gendarme, and even fellow Kurds who sided with the Turkish forces as "village guards."[249]

Then, in April 1991, Turkish President Özal initiated a landmark national discussion on the existence of Kurds, the approaches taken towards Kurdish political demands, and abrogated the law prohibiting public use of the Kurdish language.[250] Nicole Watts explains the timing for this development as an outcome of the end of the Cold War, when renewed attention on Turkey's role as a democratic model forced Turkish state representatives "into the awkward position of trying to explain to the international community why Turkish democracy necessitated repression of Kurdish political identity,"[251] all of which was questioned in the context of Turkey's aspiration to become a member of the European Community. Subsequently, at the same time that the state carried out a serious and indiscriminate offensive against the Kurds, in the 1990s, "promoting the notion of specifically Kurdish cultural rights" became a "standard litany for

247. Brenda Campbell and Michael Ivers, "Indiscriminate Use of Force: Violence in South-east Turkey Fact-Finding Mission Report," KHRP and Bar Human Rights Committee of England and Wales, October 2006, p. 12, note 6.

248. KHRP, "Trial Observation Report, Turkey's Shame," p. 28. Several human rights organizations including: Amnesty International, Human Rights Watch, Kurdish Human Rights Project (KHRP), and the İHD thoroughly documented these incidents.

249. KHRP, "Trial Observation Report, Turkey's Shame," p. 28.

250. Fuller, "The Fate of the Kurds," p. 114. Although the official ban on Kurdish language was lifted in April 1991, it was in November 1991 that Leyla Zana used one sentence of Kurdish in the Turkish parliament, which became grounds for the accusation against her that she was a traitor to the state and needed to be removed from political office.

251. Watts, "Pro-Kurdish Parties," p. 635.

a wide array of Turkish civic and state actors, from Islamist political parties to business organizations, human-rights groups, prime ministers, and mainstream newspaper columnists."[252] By the mid-1990s, both international and domestic discourse on Turkey's claim as a democratic state began to hinge upon the country's treatment of its Kurds. Against this tumultuous background, in this time period it is possible to see Kurdish women organizing — in a variety of ways — speaking out against abuse, violence, and discrimination perpetrated by the state as well as within their community.

As discussed in the chapter dealing with women and the PKK, initially, the Kurdish national movement of the 1980s became "the guarantor of women's autonomy," but also sought "to determine the content of this autonomy," which posed a challenge to the "agency of women in the construction of female identity, independently."[253] Although this held true in the mid-1980s (see the early, limited involvement of women in the PKK), the rapidly expanding dimensions and scope of the national struggle, coupled with the advancements in the Turkish women's rights movement that extended to Kurdish women, enabled Kurdish women to create a space for themselves and to step into powerful roles of leadership relatively quickly.

Due to the fact that Kurdish political leaders needed as much support from the Kurds as possible, by the 1990s Kurdish women were able to dictate their terms of involvement beyond the original boundaries considered appropriate for their participation. They began to challenge persistent misogynistic and patriarchal practices, questioned the inconsistencies in the struggle's rhetoric, and realized the need to specifically address the rights of women in Kurdish society as an essential means in the pursuit of national liberation. By the mid to late 1990s, they began to receive increasing support for their actions from Kurdish men, and particularly from Kurdish political leadership.

The Story of Leyla Zana: the Trailblazer

In addition to the cadres of female PKK fighters, other Kurdish women, like Leyla Zana, the first Kurdish woman elected to the Turkish parliament, have pursued alternative avenues to fight the battle for recognition of the Kurdish national identity in Turkey. Interestingly, although never a member of the PKK herself, Leyla Zana attributes the participation of women and, indirectly, her own involvement in the Kurdish nation building movement to the incorporation

---

252. Ibid., p. 631.
253. Dryaz, "Women and Nationalism: How Women Activists are Changing the Kurdish Conflict."

of women into the PKK and to Öcalan's ideological commitment to gender equality. In her view, the PKK-initiated struggle for recognition and rights, with its explicit inclusion of women and vision for Kurdish women to gain women's rights, not only fortified the national struggle but also propelled Kurdish women into a period of rapid transformation. Prior to this renaissance, she claims, women accepted a fate of servitude, both to their male counterparts as well as to their situation in Turkey.[254] However, in the 1980s, when she discovered that Kurdish women were carrying guns, Leyla Zana said, "I was moved to action. This changes everything, I told myself, a woman is also a human being."[255] As previously discussed, though, not only the PKK enabled Kurdish women to expand their political activities, which ultimately led to organizing beyond the national struggle in a parallel pursuit of Kurdish women's rights. Leyla Zana's political career is testament to this claim.

Until 1980, Leyla Zana described her life as a long pursuit of "Turkishness," since to be a Kurd was a disgrace.[256] Born in 1961 to an illiterate mother in a traditional family, she spent the first 15 years of her life in a village called Silvan in the district of Baçe, located in eastern Turkey.[257] She attended elementary school for a year and a half at which time her father, who did not believe in educating girls, stopped her from continuing.[258] Further impeding her ability to study, Turkish was the language of instruction at the school she attended, a struggle shared by a majority of Kurdish women in that time period and still today. As a rural Kurdish girl, she had not learned to speak Turkish and, as part of state policy, she was forbidden to speak her native Kurdish dialect.[259] The combination of these two factors made Leyla Zana's studies impossible.

Considered a rebel since childhood, Leyla Zana was defiant of orthodox religious practice and the male-dominated social order that pervaded her upbringing.[260] Despite a spirited nature and a pronounced sense of justice, she could not escape the milieu from which she came. What resources, after all, could a young, illiterate Kurdish woman call upon to remove herself from the environment in which she was raised? At the age of 14 Leyla's father arranged for her to marry his cousin, Mehdi Zana, a man 20 years her senior. Reflecting

---

254. Zana, *Writings from Prison* (Watertown, Massachussetts: Blue Crane Books, 1999), p. 56.
255. Kutschera, "A Silent Scream," pp. 33–35.
256. Ibid., p. 33.
257. Zana, *Writings from Prison*, p. 56.
258. Ibid., p. xxiii.
259. Aysegul Sert, "A Woman, A Kurd, and An Optimist," *The New York Times*: The Female Factor, February 19, 2013, accessed February 22, 2013.
260. Zana, *Writings from Prison*, p. xxiii.

on her marriage to Mehdi, Leyla Zana said, "I did not choose my husband and I knew that my life from then on would be a difficult one."[261] The relationship shared between Mehdi and Leyla, however, foreshadowed the subtle socio-political and cultural changes that began in the 1980s for the Kurds of Turkey that soon affected Kurdish women as well. Accounts given by Leyla Zana regarding her husband's influence on her life as a Kurdish nationalist and rights activist vary, from anecdotes describing him as supportive of her self-advancement, to those that indicate he was antagonistic to her activities and controlling in the traditional sense of wedlock in Kurdish society. Shortly after their wedding, Leyla and Mehdi relocated to Diyarbakır where, in 1976, she gave birth to her son, Ronay; in the following year, Mehdi became mayor-elect of Diyarbakır.[262] While her husband pursued his political career and, later, in his absence, Leyla Zana learned Turkish and, encouraged by Mehdi, became the first woman in Diyarbakır to receive a high school equivalency diploma without actually attending school.[263] In an interview from 1993, however, Leyla Zana revealed that during the first five years of marriage her life "was not her own"; it was controlled by Mehdi, and Leyla's main purpose was to please her husband. Moreover, until 1980, she states it was not the custom of her husband or the politicians of his generation to mix family life with political life.[264] In the early years of their marriage, she was mainly confined to the house in a big city, detached from her family and familiar surroundings.

Following the 1980 military coup, when oppression and persecution of the Kurds at the hands of the Turkish authorities surged, Mehdi Zana was accused of separatism, arrested, tortured, and thrown in prison to serve a 30-year sentence. Pregnant with her daughter, Ruken, Leyla Zana followed her husband from prison to prison, campaigning for his release. In the process of working toward her husband's release, unbeknownst to her, Leyla Zana began to redirect the course of her life.[265]

In 1984, four years after Mehdi Zana's incarceration, the PKK's declaration of war led Turkey's leaders to identify the group as public enemy number one, to spare no resources to defeat the organization, and to suppress the Kurds of Turkey as a whole, regardless of whether or not they were affiliated with the PKK. In those chaotic first years of the insurgency and Mehdi Zana's imprisonment, Leyla Zana became the unofficial spokesperson for women

261. Kutschera, "A Silent Scream," p. 33.
262. Ibid., p. xxiii.
263. Ibid., p. xxiv.
264. Kutschera, "A Silent Scream," p. 33.
265. Jiyar Gol, "Turkey-Kurdish Woman, Leyla Zana," Short Documentary, Jiyar Films, 2006, accessed May 2, 2011.

whose husbands shared his fate.[266] Her efforts included visits to Mehdi and other Kurdish prisoners and demonstrations outside prison walls where Kurdish men were serving sentences. On these occasions, she met with Kurdish men and women seeking justice and freedom for their incarcerated family members. Consequently, her interactions with fellow Kurds inspired Zana to question her own identity and what it meant to be a Kurd. She began taking part in political activities on her own accord and held strikes in front of the prison.[267]

As she became aware of the widespread devastation wreaked upon Kurdish women due to the conflict, Leyla Zana extended her political efforts beyond advocating for her husband's release and the Kurdish cause to include the promotion of women's rights. Also, continued challenges from within Leyla Zana's community to her political activities based on her womanhood opened her eyes to the need to promote Kurdish women's rights as vigorously as national rights. In order to carry out this work, she founded and chaired a women's group that opened branches in Diyarbakır and Istanbul, and worked for a human rights association in Diyarbakır. Indeed, quite quickly, Leyla Zana recognized the developmentally debilitating effects of both Kurdish and Turkish societies' view that "If you are a man, you have value; if you are a woman, you don't. [And] [t]his narrow-mindedness had to be shattered."[268]

Throughout this restive period, separated from family and friends, Leyla Zana was forced to think and act for herself for the first time.[269] She became acquainted with the power of her unmitigated agency and her talent for defying status quo, both as a politicized Kurd and as a Kurdish woman. As she became an increasingly public figure, Leyla observed that Mehdi wanted her to be politically involved, but for his own purposes. In her own words: "he was not happy when I did something for me," but she was able to tell herself, "Here I am. I do exist."[270] Her self-transformation had already occurred, and so her work continued.

In 1988, another poignant experience reinforced Leyla Zana's determination to serve as a leader in her people's struggle. According to Leyla's recounting of the incident, during an attempt to visit Mehdi in prison in July, she joined a group of anxious and overheated elderly and young people, and women carrying fussy, uncomfortable babies, accompanied by small children. After waiting many hours, the prison guards led the group into a garden where they were told visiting privileges would not be granted on that day. From the other

---

266. Zana, *Writings from Prison*, p. xxiv.
267. Ibid., p. xxiv.
268. Sert, "A Kurd, A Woman and Optimist," *New York Times.*
269. Zana, *Writings from Prison*, p. xxiv.
270. Kutschera, "A Silent Scream," p. 33.

side of the wall separating the infuriated crowd from the prisoners, they could hear the cries of men being beaten — the men they came to see. A riot ensued after which 83 people were arrested, including Leyla Zana, who was accused by a soldier of trying to take his gun and inciting revolt.[271]

During the first week of imprisonment, she was beaten, tortured, and sexually abused. Instead of being shattered and defeated, for Leyla Zana, the 50 days spent sharing a cell with "common prisoners, thieves, prostitutes and drug addicts" marked the time that she became a political activist.[272] In the years leading up to her second jail term (1994), multiple attempts on her life and death threats purportedly orchestrated by the Turkish secret services, only solidified her resolve to tackle injustice.[273] In fact, the more effort the authorities expended on silencing her, the more she was motivated to effect change.

In this tenuous atmosphere, Leyla Zana stepped up her political involvement in the Kurdish issue by running for a seat in the Turkish Grand National Assembly (TBMM) elections of 1991, a privilege afforded to her as a citizen of Turkey. She was elected by 84 percent of her district in Diyarbakır[274] on the ticket of the Social Democrat Populist Party's (SHP — Sosyal Demokrat Halkçi Parti), a political faction that promoted a platform of "commitment to the deepening of democracy in Turkey" and supported a political solution (as opposed to a military solution) to the Kurdish question "if the political conditions were right." In the early 1990s the SHP shared an agenda and therefore engaged in a complicated relationship with the first legal Kurdish party in Turkey, the People's Labor Party (HEP — Halkın Emek Partisi; established in March 1990).[275] For the HEP, campaigning with the SHP for democratic reform helped the Kurdish party to appeal to a broader Turkish audience beyond the Kurds. Consequently, common ground led Kurdish political leaders to run on SHP tickets.[276]

During Leyla Zana's first day in office she sought to make good on her promises to her supporters and their shared struggle for equal rights as Kurdish citizens of Turkey.[277] To that effect, in addition to the ceremonial and mandatory

---

271. Ibid.
272. Ibid., p. 34.
273. Zana, *Writings from Prison*, p. 8.
274. van Bruinessen, "From Adela Khanum to Leyla Zana," p. 106.
275. Martin van Bruinessen, "Turkey's Death Squads," *Middle East Report*, No. 99, Turkey: Insolvent Ideologies, Fractured State, (April–June 1996), Middle East Research and Information Project (MERIP), p. 20.
276. Cengiz Gunes, *The Kurdish National Movement: From Protest to Resistance* (New York: Routledge, 2012), pp.156–160.
277. Zana, *Writings from Prison*, p. xxiv.

declaration of a loyalty oath to the Republic of Turkey at her invocation
ceremony on November 6, 1991, Leyla Zana, the first Kurdish woman to be
elected to the Turkish parliament, concluded her recitation with the following
sentence:

> "I underwent that formality under duress. I will fight for the
> fraternal coexistence of the Kurdish and Turkish peoples within
> the context of democracy."[278]

She spoke these words in her Kurdish mother tongue, a prohibited language
since the establishment of the Turkish state, reinforced in 1982, when the
redrafted Turkish Constitution declared Turkish as the mother tongue of Turkey
as opposed to the official language of all Turkish citizens.[279] She did this against
the background of the military junta's Law No. 2932 (1983), which banned the
use of Kurdish language in Turkey, even in private, that lasted until 1991, just
six months before Zana was sworn into office.[280] Proving the shallow nature of
Prime Minister Turgut Özal's reform policy regarding the legality of the use
of Kurdish language, Leyla Zana's direct challenge to the state's institutional
denial of Kurdish language and ethnicity marked the first protest made in
the parliamentary body by one of its own members against Turkey and its
constitution.[281]

Seconds after her statement the Turkish Grand National Assembly exploded
into a cacophony of slanderous epithets. "There were cries of 'separatist!',
'traitor!', 'arrest her!' and even 'hang her!', and legal proceedings were
immediately initiated."[282] Amidst the uproar caused by her addendum to the
loyalty oath, Zana and her fellow Kurdish deputies were labeled, collectively, as
a terrorist cell.[283]

Following her controversial action, in November 1991, SHP leadership
asked Leyla Zana to resign.[284] Nevertheless, she refused to leave the party until
a year later when, on March 21, 1992, 100 Kurdish civilians were massacred
for holding a Kurdish New Year's demonstration in Cizre, a Kurdish-majority

---

278. Ibid., p. 2.
279. Watts, "Pro-Kurdish Parties," p. 635.
280. International Free Women's Foundation, *Psychological Consequences*, p. 29.
281. Zana, *Writings from Prison*, p. 13.
282. Amnesty International, "TURKEY: The colours of their clothes: parliamentary
    deputies serve 15 years' imprisonment for expressions of Kurdish political identity."
    Amnesty International, December 1997, AI Index: EUR44/85/97.
283. Gol, "Turkey-Kurdish Woman, Leyla Zana," Short Documentary.
284. Kutschera, "A Silent Scream," p. 35.

city located in southeastern Turkey.[285] The massacre in Cizre was the breaking
point for Leyla Zana and her colleagues, and a clear indication that the SHP
leadership was not willing to put meaningful pressure on the government to
solve the Kurdish problem. After this incident, Leyla Zana and 20 other Kurdish
members of parliament tendered their resignation from the SHP for its inaction
in the aftermath of the massacre, and joined the HEP.[286]

Zana's persistent outspokenness against the political and cultural
discrimination of the Kurdish people made her into a pariah among her
parliamentary colleagues. Feeling alienated and powerless, and unable to
take the floor for her politically subversive actions and the disdain harbored
against her by the members of many other political parties, Leyla Zana turned
to Western media and leaders to promote the plight of her people. Taking
advantage of her parliamentary immunity, she organized tours for invited
foreign leaders and members of the press to witness the policy of evacuation
and destruction of Kurdish villages implemented by the Turkish government
in its war against the PKK[287] that, at the time, was in its tenth year of armed
resistance against the Turkish army.[288]

Leyla Zana advocated for Kurdish rights abroad, in person, as well. On
May 17, 1993, she was invited to Washington D.C. to brief members of the U.S.
Congress, and to speak at the Carnegie Endowment for International Peace.
At these hearings she spoke of the demolition of Kurdish villages and the
degradation of the Kurdish people, and of the ineptitude of both the Turkish and
Kurdish political leaderships to deal with the Kurdish question in a productive
manner.[289] She and her colleagues also organized a diplomatic tour covering
Europe that included Germany, England, and the Scandinavian countries of
Northern Europe.[290]

According to Leyla Zana, the extensive press coverage given to her meetings
with high-level contacts contributed to the internationalization of the Kurdish
problem in Turkey.[291] Meanwhile in Turkey, Zana's Turkish co-parliamentarians
viewed her rising international notoriety on the Kurdish question as a severe
national threat, and began to build their case against Zana and her colleagues.
The first concrete action against her took place in July 1993 in the Constitutional

---

285. Zana, *Writings from Prison*, p. 3.

286. Ibid.

287. Ibid., pp. 4–5.

288. Ali Kemal Özcan, *Turkey's Kurds: A Theoretical Analysis of the PKK and Abdullah
      Öcalan*, (London and New York: Routledge, Taylor & Francis Group, 2006), p. 18.

289. Zana, *Writings from Prison*, p. xxv.

290. Ibid., p. 5.

291. Ibid.

Court, which banned the HEP on accusation and charge of being a mouthpiece for the PKK. In order to stay active at the national legislative level, Leyla Zana and her fellow deputies immediately founded the Democracy Party (DEP — Demokrasi Partisi).[292]

Nevertheless, during early spring 1994, a majority parliamentary vote lifted the immunity of all members that took part in the diplomatic delegations organized by Zana.[293] On a number of charges, Leyla Zana and her Kurdish colleagues — Hatip Dicle, Orhan Doğan, and Salim Sadak — were stripped of parliamentary immunity and arrested. According to the prosecution, the accused were guilty of separatism and illegal activities by having expressed Kurdish identity in Parliament, demonstrated by the color of their clothes and, by Zana, in the colors of her hair accessories on the day she took oath in office.[294] On June 16, 1994, the Constitutional Court outlawed the DEP.[295] By December 1994, a panel of Turkish civil and military judges convicted Leyla Zana and her four colleagues, and sentenced each to 15 years in prison.[296]

Immediately adopted by Amnesty International as a prisoner of conscience, the story of Leyla Zana became a high-profile international affair.[297] Her relationship with members of the U.S. Congress and François Mitterand, former President of France and, especially, his wife Danielle Mitterand, ensured her case's public reputation. Moreover, while serving her prison sentence, Leyla Zana was nominated for and received, in absentia, several prestigious international prizes. She was awarded the Raftos Prize for Human Rights from Norway (1994), the Bruno Kreisky Peace Prize from Austria (1995), the Aix-la-Chappelle International Peace Prize from Germany (1995), the Sakharov Prize for Freedom of Thought from the European Parliament (1995), and the Women of the Year Prize from the Val d'Aosta Regional Council of Northern Italy (1998); and she was nominated for the Nobel Peace Prize three times between 1995 and 1998.[298] Even from prison, her efforts on behalf of the Kurdish people kept her role in the struggle relevant.

In a statement she intended to read on December 8, 1994, during the final hearing of her trial in Ankara when the Turkish government finally managed to remove her from the public eye, Leyla Zana proclaimed:

---

292. Watts, "Pro-Kurdish Parties," p. 631.

293. Zana, *Writings from Prison*, p. 5.

294. Ibid., p. xxv.

295. Watts, "Pro-Kurdish Parties," p. 632.

296. Zana, *Writings from Prison*, p. xxv.

297. Amnesty International, "TURKEY: The Color of Their Clothes," p. 1.

298. Zana, *Writings from Prison*, p. xxv.

"Only fourteen years ago Leyla Zana was an ordinary young peasant girl whose world was limited to the search for a little domestic happiness. The events that followed the coup d'etat [of 1980] and the barbarities she suffered have made her an activist with a will of steel. Were you to burn or hang her, there would be millions of Kurdish women, tens of thousands of Leyla Zanas, who would rise up before you and carry on the struggle."[299]*

After serving one decade of her sentence, a retrial process opened in April 2003, which resulted in another 15-year prison term for Leyla Zana and her colleagues. Then, suddenly, on June 9, 2004, they were released from prison by order of a Turkish appeals court.[300] It is believed that Zana's release came after repeated warnings from European institutions that the continued imprisonment of the four Kurdish legislators would impede Turkey's efforts to join the European Union.[301] Wasting no time, four months after her release, Leyla Zana announced the establishment of the Democratic Society Party (DTP — Demokratik Toplum Partisi), the vehicle through which she and her colleagues would honor their commitment to the pursuit of democracy and peace in order to bring about the improvement in the plight of the Kurds in Turkey. On the same day, Leyla Zana appeared in court for yet another hearing before an Ankara court that sought to overturn the annulled convictions that secured her release, a move that failed.[302]

In 2009, the Turkish Constitutional Court slapped Leyla Zana with a five-year ban from politics for her affiliation with the DTP, which the government dissolved by citing alleged ties to the PKK.[303] Never one to be deterred by government intimidation, in the June 2011 Turkish national elections, Leyla Zana and ten other Kurdish female candidates won seats in the TBMM.[304] They were able to do so under the auspices of the pro-Kurdish Peace and Democracy

299. Ibid., p. 34; *In protest of the sham trial she received, Leyla Zana's lawyers boycotted her last hearing and thus, she decided not read the text in court.
300. Amnesty International, "VICTORY: Leyla Zana — Special Focus Case," Amnesty International, June 9, 2004, accessed May 22, 2012.
301. Jonathan Sugden and Sunar Yurdatapan, "Kurdish Political Leader Leyla Zana Released After Decade in Jail," Democracy Now!, June 4, 2010, accessed April 18, 2013.
302. Al-Jazeera, "Kurdish Activist to Form New Party," Al-Jazeera, Archive, October 22, 2004, accessed July 10, 2011.
303. Daily Sabah, "Political Ban of Pro-Kurdish Politicians Ends as They Seek to Join HDP," Daily Sabah, Politics, accessed January 28, 2015.
304. "12 Haziran'da seçilen kadın milletvekilleri 'rekor' kırdı," BBC Türkçe, June 13, 2011, accessed June 22, 2011.

Party (BDP — Barış ve Demokrasi Partisi) that decided to field independent candidates during the 2011 elections.[305] In doing so, the BDP overcame the 10 percent threshold in Turkey's proportional-representation system — a stipulation that precludes smaller parties from entering the Parliament.[306] Zana and her fellow independents secured 62.08 percent of the Kurdish vote in the Diyarbakır district.[307] On October 1, 2011, she was sworn-in as a member of the Turkish parliament, stating that what had once more brought her to the podium of the Turkish National Assembly was her belief in peace.[308] On May 24, 2012, Leyla Zana was again sentenced to prison for allegedly spreading pro-PKK propaganda in a series of speeches she made in 2008. Similar to her situation in 1991, though, as long as Zana remains a member of parliament, she enjoys parliamentary immunity.[309]

Characteristic of her leadership, determination, and perseverance in the face of intimidation, three weeks after the pronouncement of a ten-year prison sentence, she gave an interview to *Hürriyet Daily News* reaffirming her dedication to justice through political change. On June 14, 2012, Zana iterated that Prime Minister Erdoğan is the only Turkish leader capable of facilitating a peaceful resolution to the Kurdish issue and that she hoped to meet with him to discuss the matter.[310] On June 30, 2012, Erdoğan and Zana met face-to-face, eliciting mixed reactions from suspicious and confused Turkish political factions as well as the BDP. During a ninety-minute meeting, Zana's main message to the Turkish leader was to focus on implementing democratic reforms that would expand the rights and liberties of the Kurds, and recognize them as a distinct people within Turkey. She praised him for the measures he implemented in the "Kurdish Opening" that began in 2009, and asked that he continue this approach as opposed to the "security-priority" agenda pursued in 2011 and 2012, which

---

305. Kurd Net, "Former Prominent Kurdish Legislator Leyla Zana Hoping to Make Comeback in Turkey's June Elections," *Kurd Net*, April 11, 2011, accessed April 11, 2011.
306. Ayla Albayrak and JoeParkinson, "Turkey Reinstates Kurdish Candidates," *The Wall Street Journal*, April 22, 2011, accessed April 24, 2011.
307. Institut Kurde de Paris, "Information and Liaison Bulletin, No. 315, June 2011," Institute Kurde de Paris, June 2011, accessed December 23, 2011.
308. *Radikal*, "Yine Vekil " ("Representative Wants More"), *Radikal*, accessed October 2, 2011.
309. Daren Butler, "Turkish Court Convicts Turkish Politician Over Speeches," *Reuters News Service*, May 24, 2012, accessed July 9, 2012.
310. *Hürriyet Daily News*, "Turkish PM Erdogan, Zana to Meet to Discuss Kurdish Issue."

detracted from what Zana deemed as the start of positive developments vis-à-vis the Kurds of Turkey.[311]

The strange predicament in which Leyla Zana found herself in 2012 — prooocuted as an enemy of the state one month, then received by the prime minister in a high-profile, closed-door meeting 37 days later, and lauded by the Turkish leader as a true negotiator for peace — illustrates the unique situation of Kurdish women in Turkey who still struggle, but also now deftly maneuver within the Turkish political system. In yet another episode of Leyla Zana's tumultuous and fraught relationship with the Turkish government, December 2014 marked the end of Zana's five-year ban political ban. Shortly thereafter, Zana announced her intention to join the 2012-established, pro-Kurdish Peoples' Democratic Party (HDP — Halkların Demokratik Partisi), an alliance party to the BDP.[312]

For Kurdish women, Leyla Zana's story is a testament to the achievements in empowerment Kurdish women have earned in an ongoing, double-sided struggle as Kurds and as women, within a dynamic and changing Turkey. As second-class citizens, both as Kurds and as women, women like Leyla Zana and her cohorts have been at a severe disadvantage within the Turkish state since its inception in the 1920s, and within Kurdish society for centuries. Yet, within that same Turkish state, Zana, an illiterate, Kurdish peasant girl from the Southeast became a political activist, a journalist, a women's rights advocate, a parliamentarian, an internationally renowned figure, a political prisoner, and a parliamentarian once again. Of course, Leyla Zana's story is but one of many courageous biographies of trailblazing Kurdish women ensuring that the Kurdish women's rights movement will continue to advance.

---

311. *Hürriyet Daily News*, "Zana reveals details of Erdogan meeting," *Hürriyet Daily News*, July 12, 2012, accessed July 15, 2012.

312. *Daily Sabah*, "Political Ban of Pro-Kurdish Politicians Ends as They Seek to Join HDP."

Chapter 7

Kurdish Women of Turkey Forge Ahead

The ongoing ethno-national movement and its inclusion of women are largely responsible for the empowerment of Kurdish women. Ultimately, however, credit for the continued efforts to advance Kurdish women's political, social, civil, economic, and gender rights must be apportioned to Kurdish women themselves, who have dedicated and risked their lives and reputations for future generations of Kurdish women to enjoy a more just and equitable future. Indubitably, over the past 30 years the Kurdish women of Turkey have done nothing less than instigate a social revolution.

Kurdish Women in Pursuit of Political Influence and Change

On the political front, in the late 1990s, Kurdish political factions established separate women and youth branches to foster the wider mobilization of Kurdish society into the pro-Kurdish political movement.[313] Since then, Kurdish political leaders and their parties have pursued an aggressive policy of inclusion in public events and quotas for women. For the first time, three Kurdish women were elected as local mayors in Turkey in 1999.[314] Until the People's Democracy Party (Halkın Demokrasi Partisi) was banned in 2003, its women's branch encouraged the participation of women in civil society by sponsoring local festivals and International Women's Day marches — providing housewives who were not politically active an opportunity for public political engagement.[315] In 2004, under pressure from its women's branch, the leadership of the Democratic People's Party (DEHAP — Demokratik Halk Partisi; the successor to Halkın Demokrasi Partisi) agreed to a gender quota system of 40 percent for women

---

313. Gunes, *The Kurdish National Movement*, p. 164.
314. Gültan Kışanak, Nadje Al-Ali, and Latif Tas, "Kurdish women's battle continues against state and patriarchy, says first female co-mayor of Diyarbakir. Interview," *Open Democracy*, August 12, 2016, accessed on August 14, 2016.
315. Secor, "There is an Istanbul," p. 365.

and the inclusion of a female co-presidential position for every presidential office held by a male.[316] The pro-Kurdish Peace and Democracy Party's (BDP, DTP's successor) official party protocol dictates that a woman must be one of its two chairs.[317] On September 4, 2011, MP Gültan Kışanak — a veteran Kurdish female activist, journalist and political organizer — was elected as the female co-chair of the BDP alongside the reelected MP Selahattin Demirtaş.[318] According to Kışanak, the first woman elected to the position of co-mayor of Diyarbakir/ Amed (in 2014), women in the position of co-chair were initially perceived as assistants to their male counterparts. In 2007, when eight out of 26 Kurdish MPs were women, this perception began to change as Kurdish women "became more confident as co-chairs and men had to except them as equals."[319]

As of 2014, out of the 26 female mayors throughout Turkey (out of 2,964),[320] 14 were BDP members.[321] Comparatively, there was only one female mayor from the National Movement Party (MHP — Milliyetçi Hareket Partisi), and the remaining 11 came from the ruling-Justice and Development Party (AKP — Adalet ve Kalkınma Partisi) and the Republican People's Party (CHP — Cumhuriyet Halk Partisi).[322] In addition, the BDP women's quota requires that if a party mayor is male, his deputy will be female.[323] In the March 2014 local elections, the practice of co-ed leadership spread to most BDP local races.[324]

316. Dryaz, "Women and Nationalism: How Women Activists are Changing the Kurdish Conflict."

317. "Kurdish women fight for rights of both groups, Istanbul deputy says," *Hürriyet Daily News*, June 30, 2010.

318. "BDP's Second Congress: Is the Destination Ankara or is it Kurdistan?," *The Kurdish Globe*, September 10, 2011, accessed October 1, 2011.

319. Kışanak, Gültan, Nadje Al-Ali, and Latif Tas, "Kurdish Women's Battle Continues Against State and Patriarchy, Says First Female Co-mayor of Diyarbakir. Interview."

320. Yonca Poyraz Doğan, "Turkish Women Face Discrimination, Violence, Illiteracy Despite Small Gains," *Today's Zaman*, March 7, 2012, accessed April 22, 2013.

321. *Hürriyet Daily News*, "Kurdish Women Fight for Rights of Both Groups..."

322. Meral Tamet, "Can Erdogan Make Room for Women in the AKP Congress," *Al-Monitor*, September 28, 2012, accessed April 22, 2013. Original article, "Can Prime Minister Open up Space for Women in AKP Congress?," published by *Milliyet* (Turkish) and translated by Timur Goksel.

323. "KURDISTAN: Kurdish Women in Southeast Turkey Grow Strong Support Networks," originally printed in *Hürriyet Daily News*, December 10, 2010, accessed from *Peacewomen.org*: accessed April 22, 2011.

324. Bernard, "Women and the Kurdish Movement in Turkey," p. 4.

Of the 28 female parliamentary members elected in the June 2011 Turkish national elections, 11 were Kurdish.[325] Over thirty percent of the BDP candidates for parliament were women.[326] While the BDP led in the ratios for "gender equality" in elections, its female leaders remained disappointed in not having reached the 33 percent party quota. (Allegedly, AKP leader and President Erdoğan continue to fight for a 20 percent women's quota; the MHP refuses to have such a quota; and the CHP adopted a 33 percent quota after the 2011 elections.)[327] In the 2015 Turkish national elections, the pro-Kurdish HDP surpassed the 10 percent threshold by securing 13 percent of the national vote, and put 31 female candidates into the TNMM, a higher percentage of women than any other party that secured seats in the election.[328] The HDP is also the only political party in Turkey to ever include a "declaration on women" in its organizational documents, to label itself a "women's party," and to include in its campaign platform a promise to establish a women's ministry to address gendercide and institutional gender discrimination.[329]

Another high profile female Kurd is Aysel Tuğluk, a graduate of the Istanbul University Law Faculty who became Öcalan's personal attorney.[330] She is a founding member of the Patriotic Women's Association, and served as the co-president of the Democratic Society Party (DTP; DEHAP's successor),[331] which, in 2006, engaged in comprehensive strategies to combat violence against women in Kurdish communities.[332] She was elected to the Turkish parliament in 2008.[333] As of 2013, she also served as the co-chair of DÖKH (Demokratik Özgür Kadın Hareketi — Democratic and Free Women Movement), an umbrella Kurdish women's rights and lobbying group founded by Kurdish women in Turkey

325. "12 Haziran'da seçilen kadın milletvekilleri 'rekor' kırdı," ("On June 12 the Record for Elected Women MPs is Broken"), *BBC* Turkey.
326. Çağaptay, "Women 'Appear' in Turkey's Parliament."
327. Tamet, "Can Erdoğan Make Room for Women in the AKP Congress," *Al-Monitor*.
328. Michael Pizzi, "Kurdish Election Gains are 'Historic' Boost for Inclusion in Turkey," *Al-Jazeera* America, June 9, 2015, accessed October 12, 2015.
329. Semanur Karaman, "Turkey Elections Mark the Start of a Revolution for Women," *The Guardian*, June 19, 2015, accessed October 12, 2015.
330. *Hürriyet Daily News*, "DTP Also to Blame in Kurdish Problem, Says Deputy," *Hürriyet Daily News*, July 29, 2009, accessed February 5, 2011.
331. Gunes, *The Kurdish National Movement in Turkey*, p. 164.
332. International Free Women's Foundation, *Psychological Trauma*, p. 41.
333. Aysel Tuğluk, "Dersim 1938: 70 Years After," a conference hosted by Feleknas Unca and sponsored by the European United Left/Nordic Green Left Parliamentary Group and the European Parliament, November 13, 2008, 3pm-6:30 pm, EP, ASP 1G3, accessed January 12, 2012.

in 2003.[334] At the time of writing, Tuğluk's DÖKH co-chair was BDP co-chair Gültan Kışanak.[335]

Since her election to parliament, in addition to the work Tuğluk pursues for the Kurds and for Kurdish women, she has constantly battled accusations by the Turkish authorities for alleged separatist activities. In 2009, she received an 18-month prison sentence for a speech made on May 16, 2006, for which she was accused of supporting the PKK. Although legal proceedings against her began in 2006, her parliamentary immunity prevented the trial's continuation. Nevertheless, in a legal precedent, Turkey violated its own constitution when, prior to the end of her term, a Diyarbakır court convicted Tuğluk in February 2009, citing anti-terrorist laws as justification of her conviction.[336] Additionally, along with Leyla Zana and 28 other politicians, the five-year political ban on party affiliation decreed by the Turkish Constitutional Court in 2009 also included Tuğluk.[337]

In August 2011, Tuğluk was convicted by another Turkish court for the dissemination of propaganda for the PKK in a speech she made in southeastern Turkey on March 17, 2010. Based on the fact that she was re-elected as an independent, BDP-backed candidate to the parliament by the Kurdish-populated Van District in June 2011, it is clear that MP Aysel Tuğluk, who is also co-chair of the pro-Kurdish Democratic Society Congress, did not feel threatened by the Turkish authorities and the attempts to stifle her advocacy for the Kurdish people.[338] In June 2012, she was sentenced to 14.5 years in prison, on charges of "making propaganda for a terrorist organization" and "engaging in crimes on

---

334. "Demokratik Özgür Kadın Hareketi kuruldu," SAVAS KARSITLARI, September 18, 2003, accessed April 25, 2013. Following a three-day conference held in Istanbul, Turkey, September 13-15, 2003, 198 delegates representing several Kurdish women's rights organizations voted to form the umbrella organization, DÖKH, to carry out lobbying activities for peace until legislation in support of the women's movement came into being. DÖKH strives for women's full participation in society, including political and economic opportunities, and also seeks to put Kurdish women in local leadership positions so that policy addressing Kurdish women's issues can be formed and implemented in an efficient manner.

335. DÖKH (Demokratik Özgür Kadın Hareketi), "Call for Participation DÖKH's 1st Middle East Women's Conference Amed (Diyarbakır), Turkey, 31 May-2 June 2013," Association for Women's Rights in Development (AWID), March 13, 2013, accessed April 12, 2013.

336. "Turkish Court Sentences Kurdish MP to Jail for Kurdish PKK Rebel Remarks," EKurd.net, February 5, 2009, accessed March 25, 2011.

337. I, "Political Ban of Pro-Kurdish Politicians Ends as They Seek to Join HDP."

338. "Turkish Court Sentences Kurdish Deputy Aysel Tugluk to Two Years' Jail," Kurdistan Tribune, August 2, 2011, accessed August 28, 2011.

behalf of a terrorist organization."[339] Then, in November and December of 2012, lawmakers repeatedly threatened to lift Tuğluk's parliamentary immunity and that of nine other BDP parliamentarians for "warmly embracing and chatting with armed militants of the outlawed [PKK] in the eastern province of Hakkari's Şemdinli District [on] Aug. 17."[340] As of writing, the cases against Tuğluk's are pending, but in the meantime, she remains free under parliamentary immunity.

Like most female Kurdish leaders, Tuğluk divides her political career between efforts for Kurdish political and civil rights, and the struggle for Kurdish women's rights. In 2013, she lobbied for women's rights through the vehicle of DÖKH and its regular campaigns. From May 31, to June 2, 2013, she and Gültan Kışanak coordinated DÖKH's first conference on "Middle East Women" in Diyarbakır, inviting scholars from all over the world for academic exchange on the broad theme of "'Woman, Life, Freedom' in Kurdish: '*Jin, Jiyan, Azadi*'."[341]

Yuksel Genç, a former co-chair of the DTK, who was arrested on October 31, 2011, as part of the KCK crackdown,[342] reports news of her female Kurdish colleagues in her dispatches from the Bakırkoy Prison for Women and Juveniles. She, along with Çiğdem Kılıçgün Uçar, former co-chair of BDP Istanbul; Ülker Ana, Hatice and Songul Ana, also BDP members and party administrators,[343] are but a few of the many female decision makers and influential players among the Kurds of Turkey.

Kurdish Women's Civil Society Activism and Economic Participation: Improving the Denigrated Status of Kurdish Women

Despite the advances of the women's rights movements of Turkey and the progress in Kurdish women's political representation and participation, the reality is less encouraging in day-to-day life. According to a report published

339. "Kurdish Deputy Sentenced to 14.5 Years in Prison," *Today's Zaman*, June 12, 2012, accessed August 29, 2012.

340. Goksel Bozkurt, "Turkish PM Meets Kurdish MPs on Immunity Lifting Row," *Hürriyet*, December 14, 2012, accessed April 23, 2013.

341. DÖKH (Demokratik Özgür Kadın Hareketi), "Call for Participation DÖKH's 1st Middle East Women's Conference."

342. "Former DTK Co-Chair Yuksel Genç Arrested," *ANF News Agency*, October 31, 2011, accessed February 5, 2012.

343. Yuksel Genç, "Who is Deceiving Whom?," *ANF News Agency*, January 23, 2012, accessed February 5, 2012.

by Turkish news outlet *Bianet*, in 2016, men killed 261 women in Turkey. There were 17 suicides/suicide attempts, 14 deaths under suspicious conditions, and 31 unsolved femicides. One in four women were killed for attempting to divorce; 13.5 percent of the femicides occurred in places like malls or streets. Four percent of the murders committed after perpetrators were released from or escaped from prison. Nine percent of the women were killed despite being under protection of the authorities or after filing complaints of violence. Six Syrian refugee women were killed in 2016 as well. At least 417 girls were subjected to sexual abuse; 58 percent of the incidents occurred in schools. Fifty-three percent of these girls were abused at the hands of teachers, seven percent by school staff, and seven percent by relatives. 119 rape cases were reported with eight percent of the perpetrators being repeat offenders; eight percent of these rape victims were not citizens of Turkey. 175 harassment cases were reported including physical (73 percent), exhibitionism (eight percent), digital (three percent), verbal (six percent), and ten percent took other forms of harassment; nine percent of the harassers committed these crimes before. Ten percent of the women were harassed on mass transportation and nine percent occurred in workplaces.[344]

Speaking specifically to the situation of Kurdish women, in 2008, Leyla Zana addressed the ongoing injustices suffered by Kurdish woman on her first visit to London (after her 2004 release from prison) for a women's rights conference. She mentioned early and forced marriages of girls, depression and suicide, honor killings, and forced prostitution, which Zana described as the consequences of human rights abuses at the hands of state and non-state actors alike.[345] Intertwined with the hardship of being a Kurd whose ethnic identity and rights are denied by the state, she claimed Kurdish women's issues are compounded by the lack of language rights, lack of access to an impartial justice system, illiteracy, and rampant unemployment. In turn, this disconsolate situation has directly led to an increase in domestic violence, which primarily claims women

---

344. *Bianet*, "In 2016, Men Killed 261 Women," an infographic published by with the financial support of the Friedrich Ebert Stiftung and the Swedish International Development Cooperation Agency. The data reported are based on news reports from national, local, and Internet media in Turkey between January 1, 2016 and December 31, 2016.

345. Leyla Zana, "The Role of Kurdish Women in Dialogue, Conflict Resolution, and Reconstruction for Democracy and Peace," Statement given at Seminar hosted by Organization of Women's Freedom in Iraq (OWFI), held on May 24, 2008. Garden Court Chambers, 57-60 Lincoln's Inn Fields, WC2, accessed September 12, 2011.

as its victims.[346] Adding to this is the grim reality in the predominantly Kurdish-inhabited area of southeast Turkey, where fundamental mistrust of the state and police due to years of regional unrest also deter many women from reporting violence that is often sanctioned under the guise of Kurdish customary practice.[347] Yet, even with this daunting list of challenges, it is impossible to ignore the significant and increasing Kurdish women-led activities and efforts that strive to mitigate and eradicate these problems.

As early as the mid-1990s, Kurdish women started campaigning against "sexualized violence at the hands of security forces," both domestically and internationally.[348] Accordingly, the Kurdish Human Rights Project (KHRP) published that, beginning in 2000, the number of Kurdish women reporting and seeking redress to abduction, sexual abuse, and torture saw a significant increase due to three factors. First, Kurdish women were becoming more politicized in part due to their migration to urban centers where they had greater awareness of their rights and more political-organizational opportunities. For example, the widespread publicity in Turkey and abroad over the "abduction and sexual abuse of Gülbahar Gündüz," a member of the executive board of DEHAP who was attacked in broad daylight in Istanbul in June 2003, galvanized Kurdish women to take to the streets in protest and encouraged other Kurdish women to come forward with their own experiences of abuse. Second, in their 2005 Trial Observation Report, KHRP noted that, historically, although Kurdish men prevented women from reporting their experiences of sexual abuse at the hands of state actors out of shame at the breach in honor, attitudes were beginning to change. Third, in the same time period, NGOs and "pressure groups" focused on the rise in mistreatment of women "during unofficial detentions," particularly the cases where Kurdish women were abducted, detained, and tortured without any record of these events having taken place.[349] These three factors appear to have given some Kurdish women the necessary support and confidence to come forward with their grievances and testimonies of abuse.

In the same time period, Turkey met the basic candidacy requirements for EU membership. Subsequently, the country was required to bring its legal, political, and economic system and policies into alignment with EU standards in December of 1999. This milestone was quickly seized by the women's movement in Turkey as an opportunity to solidify the efforts they had been

---

346. Leyla Zana, "The Role of Kurdish Women in Dialogue, Conflict Resolution, and Reconstruction for Democracy and Peace."
347. Human Rights Watch, "He Loves You, He Beats You," p. 6.
348. International Free Women's Foundation, *Psychological Trauma*, p. 36.
349. KHRP, "Trial Observation Report, Turkey's Shame," p. 27.

making to reform policy that affected women — including Kurdish women[350] — and to maintain momentum on the gains already made.[351]

The women's movement, which in the 1980, began to tackle violence against women and its lenient handling by the state in the name of respect for "cultural practice," witnessed concrete success at the level of state legislation. As mentioned in Chapter Four, Turkish authorities had allowed for Kurdish "customs" such as honor killings and polygamy to continue with impunity in exchange for compliance with state efforts to suppress the Kurdish national struggle, as well as used the tactic of violence against women in the state's own dealings with the Kurds. However, between 2002 and 2004, a three-year campaign led by a coalition of women's and sexual liberties groups, calling itself The Platform for the Reform of the Turkish Penal Code, sought to end the impunity by addressing the shortcomings of Turkish policy. Their efforts resulted in the adoption of a draft law to the Penal Code on September 26, 2004. Amendments were instated to prevent sentence reduction for the "killings in the name of customary law."[352]

The amendments to the Penal Code also introduced the possibility of punishing perpetrators of honor killings with a life sentence.[353] The changes also criminalized marital rape; abolished an article that allowed for a reduced sentence or suspension of an indictment if a rapist or abductor married his victim; criminalized sexual harassment in the workplace; and eliminated differentiation between virgins and non-virgins, and married and unmarried women in cases dealing with sex crimes.[354] Also in 2004, an amendment to Article 10 of the 1982 constitution added a "specific provision prohibiting discrimination on the basis of sex."[355] All of these decisions, at least on paper, augmented the responsibility of the state to the protection of the individual human rights of its female citizens. Furthermore, bringing these customarily private issues into the public sphere also helped to break down the barriers of fear and shame that kept women from seeking justice for sexual crimes committed against them. Kandiyoti claims that had it not been for EU pressure and the importance Turkey's policy makers gave

---

350. Kandiyoti, "A Tangled Web: The Politics of Gender in Turkey."

351. Ilkkaracan, "The 'Turkish Model'." As early as 1990, the efforts of women's rights activists in Turkey began to gain some ground. Specifically, in that year, the Grand National Assembly repealed Article 438 of the Turkish penal code, which stipulated a reduced sentence for an individual convicted of raping a sex-worker by one-third.

352. Kandioyti, "A Tangled Web."

353. Idlis Aybars, "Seeking Real Equality for Turkey's Women," *Common Ground News Service*, November 25, 2011, accessed November 25, 2011.

354. Kandioyti, "A Tangled Web."

355. Aybars, "Seeking real equality for Turkey's women."

to it with regard to the country's future position in the international community, reforms to the Penal Code may not have been achieved.

Additionally, in the midst of this campaign in December 2013, the Women's Working Group on the Penal Code (WWRG) had the fortune of a Turkish woman, Yakin Ertürk, serving as the UN Special Rapporteur on Violence Against Women. Taking special interest in the case of women's rights in her own country, Ertürk invited the Turkish parliament and the European Union to a dialogue on the Penal Code. This gave the Platform international visibility, which the ruling AKP tried (and failed) to prevent.[356] While AKP support for the meaningful expansion of women's rights in Turkey is debatable, in the years since the party came to power in 2002, legislation championing women's rights has been groundbreaking. According to Idil Aybars, Assistant Professor of Sociology at the Middle East Technical Institute in Ankara, the explanation for this outcome is that "gender equality is currently the cornerstone of democratization and of Turkey's bid to join the European Union,"[357] and despite its frustrations with the process, Turkey still seeks to become a part of the European Union. To that end, in May 2011 Turkey signed onto the Council of Europe Convention on Violence Against Women and Domestic Violence.[358] Consequently, now all women in Turkey have the right to access legal recourse to address violence committed against them for the first time in the country's history. For Kurdish women, although not yet necessarily improving the quality of life of the masses, these policy reforms have initiated a process in which violence against Kurdish women is impermissible under any circumstances, whether in the name of security or out of "respect" for "culture." While these mechanisms are still inadequate, in comparison to the past, they are an improvement on the lack of means available to women seeking justice.

In support of this claim, in 2006, the UNHRC mission examined the rising incidents of honor killings, domestic violence, forced and/or arranged marriages, child marriages, and the suicide rate among Kurdish females in Turkey. These alarming findings also illuminated the growing civil society-built infrastructure seeking and implementing remedies to these problems that are gaining currency within Kurdish society.[359] Currently operating in 23 centers of several provinces in eastern and southeastern Turkey, is the impressive KA-MER Foundation (Kadın Merkezi, Women's Center). KA-MER assists all women of Turkey who seek refuge from the threat of honor killings and other

---

356. Kandiyoti, "A tangled web."
357. Aybars, "Seeking real equality for Turkey's women."
358. Sussman, "Why Turkey Is Backsliding on Women's Rights."
359. International Free Women's Foundation, Psychological Trauma, p. 40.

forms of domestic violence, as well as those pursuing opportunities to become self-reliant.

The Foundation is especially active in the Kurdish regions of the country, including Van, Bitlis, Şanlıurfa, Tunceli, Diyarbakır, Hakkari, and Siirt. KA-MER reaches its target population by building and staffing centers that offer daycare, counseling, employment opportunities, and literacy courses. It also sponsors a 24-hour emergency hotline that at-risk women can contact for immediate assistance, a system that has reportedly saved hundreds of lives in the past decade. KA-MER continues to expand its services to more and more villages, where it can help women combat "poverty and male sovereignty" in the places that have been traditionally out of the state's reach. Many of KA-MER's beneficiaries manage to become self-sufficient, and the organization encourages these women to reciprocate by becoming mentors and counselors to other women who seek out KA-MER's services. Over time this model has further empowered Kurdish women to help each other, creating a network of women who are gaining practical skills that are often transferable into income-generating ventures. As Kurdish women are able to contribute to the family's income — alleviating the financial burden from the male members of their families — incidence of domestic violence declines and the eagerness to send daughters into early marriages diminishes, as losing a daughter to another family results in a loss of steady income.[360]

In 2005 KA-MER reported that men also began to utilize the hotline to mobilize police and KA-MER staff in stopping planned killings from taking place. Additionally, there were cases in which brothers, uncles, and fathers brought their female relatives to KA-MER shelters to remove them from the pending threat of an honor killing. Additionally, KA-MER reported some cases where, due to the mediation services of the Emergency Intervention Team, untangling the misunderstanding or disproving the accusation allowed many women to return to their families unscathed. The public handling of these incidents allegedly mitigated the pressure from the community on these families to carry out the killing (to restore *namus*), saving the lives of a handful of Kurdish women.[361]

KA-MER's activities continue to become more sophisticated and influential at the local and national levels. In 2010, KA-MER's 23 women's centers began interviewing women in households on the challenges they face. Approximately 57,500 women per year have spoken with KA-MER staff, illustrating the legitimacy and access KA-MER has achieved within Kurdish communities, as

---

360. Anonymous, Personal Interview, March 20, 2011.
361. KA-MER, "Who's to Blame?," pp. 3, 32, 37.

well as its growing ability to give voice to the debilitating issues that Kurdish women in Turkey continue to face. Data collected by the organization are analyzed and translated into policy recommendations and advocacy campaigns that the KA-MER network spearheads every year in hopes of improving the plight of these women.[362]

At the level of grassroots activism, it is necessary to mention the unprecedented campaign calling for state accountability for missing family members, initiated in the mid-1990s by Kurdish mothers. Starting on May 27, 1995, mothers and other female relatives of "disappeared" Kurdish men, allegedly under police custody, gathered in the Galatasaray district of Istanbul every Saturday. At the time, these women were calling on the state to recover the more than 300 lost sons and relatives who had been involved in some opposition or protest activity against the state. These Kurdish women (and their Turkish female supporters) came to be known as the Saturday Mothers (Cumtaresi Anneleri). In 1996, the International League for Human Rights, a Paris-based NGO, awarded the Carl von Ossietzky Medal to this group of women for their nonviolent protest of anti-democratic practices in Turkey.[363] As of 1998, these women sustained the longest protest in "Turkish civil life," lasting 173 weeks.[364] In September 1998, following the accusation that PKK members infiltrated the ranks of the Saturday Mothers, police harassment and round-ups led the Saturday Mothers to disband from their meeting point in the Galatasaray High School.[365]

The example of Saturday Mothers is noteworthy, not only due to the fact that these women are predominantly Kurdish, but that they are primarily mothers, not militant female-PKK members nor representing Kurdish political parties, nor women who had attended university or, necessarily, any other arena of formal education. Furthermore, according to Yeşim Arat, these women, although neither linked to other women's organizations nor feminists, exemplify "feminist modes of protest," and use their "maternal role" to give legitimacy to a "radical act." Their actions revolutionized the traditional Kurdish maternal role and created a realm in which mothers become able to represent themselves and their demands. In doing so, they have also contributed to the ongoing process of the redefinition of Turkish political culture, whereby the state is forced to become accountable to all of its citizens.[366]

362. KA-MER website, www.kamer.org.tr, accessed August 2, 2012.
363. Porter, "Disappearances — an Alarming Trend."
364. Arat, "Democracy and Women in Turkey," pp. 375–377.
365. Porter, "Disappearances — an Alarming Trend."
366. Arat, "Democracy and Women in Turkey," pp. 375–377.

In 2009 filmmaker Bijoyeta Das made a short film documenting the Saturday Mothers and discovered, after a ten-year hiatus, the group had reconvened their protest in the Galatasaray district. Saturday Mothers now includes men and women, Kurdish and non-Kurdish. According to Ayşe Yılmaz, a human rights activist interviewed in the film, she claims that one of the greatest achievements of the movement is that it is now a nation-wide effort, and mothers and family members of disappeared persons come from all over the country to join the sit-ins each Saturday. Dondu Ergin, a Kurdish mother wearing a lace-trimmed headscarf, shared with Das, "mothers are screaming, with crying hearts…we will keep asking the questions until we get answers."[367]

A few months before the June 2011 national elections, Prime Minister Erdoğan met with representatives of Saturday Mothers, after which he called for an investigation into the 1980 disappearance of political activist Cemil Kırbayır. Undertaken by the Parliamentary Human Rights Investigative Commission, which interviewed witnesses to his arrest and torture, the Commission produced a report concluding he had "died under torture in custody, and referred the case to the prosecutor in the Kars region."[368] While it is easy to attribute this incident to the political trappings of an election season, it represents a significant moment in the history of the Saturday Mothers and the decades-long struggle of the Kurds to have their grievances at the hands of Turkish authorities recognized and adjudicated. It is also meaningful that the Saturday Mothers group is a Kurdish women-led movement that is nationally and internationally renowned.

As previously mentioned, in 2003 DÖKH began its mission to unite hundreds of activist Kurdish women from civil society, women's organizations, youth groups, political parties, and local government bodies. Since its inception, it has established women's assemblies in 25 cities, women's shelters for victims of gender-based violence, 17 women's cooperatives, six women's associations, and three women's academies that provide training in gender equality for academics from all disciplines. Furthermore, DÖKH established the organization Women's Initiative for Peace in 12 towns and cities, and *JINHA*, a women's press agency. The movement also oversees the BDP's promotion of gender equality in its structure as well as its programs.[369]

In the Kurd-populated areas of Turkey, international organizations (including Kurdish diaspora women's rights advocacy groups) are actively

---

367. Bijoyeta Das, *Saturday Mothers of Turkey* (2010), hosted on the site of Women's Voices Now, accessed August 23, 2012.
368. Human Rights Watch, "Time for Justice: Ending Impunity for Killings and Disappearances in 1990s Turkey," Human Rights Watch, September 2012, p. 17, accessed September 3, 2012.
369. Bernard, "Women and the Kurdish Movement in Turkey," p. 5.

involved in exposing and finding solutions to the sobering and persistent problems that violate the human rights of Kurdish women in Turkey. Connecting Kurdish women to their counterparts abroad, technology bridges the efforts of Kurdish women's diaspora groups with those organizations and individuals within Turkey. For instance, Roj Women's Association, a Kurdish and Turkish grassroots movement based in London, was established in 2004. Through the Internet, *Rojwomen.com* brings together Kurdish women in Europe as well as women in the Kurdish regions of Syria, Iran, Iraq, and Turkey. The organization has several branches, including a political arm, that campaigns for legal and political reforms with the aim of improving the lives of Kurdish and non-Kurdish women in Turkey.[370]

Kurdish Women Action Against Honour Killing (KWAHK), a network of Kurdish and non-Kurdish activists, lawyers, and academic researchers, seeks to raise national and international awareness about the issue of violence against women in Kurdish communities, particularly honor killings "both in Kurdistan and in the Diaspora."[371] KWAHK is based in London and, along with the Kurdish Women's Organization and Radio Dengî Jinan (Women's Voice Radio), identify as feminist organizations that are independent from Kurdish political parties.[372] Another network, the Kurdish Women's Rights Watch (KWRW), is another a UK-based organization dedicated to supporting and promoting women's rights in the Kurdish community, whether in Kurdistan or in the diaspora; and now incorporates KWAHK.[373]

During the latter half of the 1990s and into the 2000s, through the publication of Kurdish women's journals,[374] it is possible to observe the articulation of a Kurdish women's feminist consciousness as well. These journals include *Roza*, *Jujin* (a combination of the Kurdish words women and hedgehog), *Jin û Jiyan* (*Woman and Life*), *Ji Bo Rizgariya Jina* (*For the Emancipation of Women*), *Yaşamda Özgür Kadın* (*Free Women in Life*, Turkish), and *Özgür Kadının Sesi* (*The Free Woman's Voice*, Turkish).[375] According to Dilşa Deniz, a founder, editorial board member, and contributor to *Jujin* and *Roza*, the goals of these publications were

---

370. "About us," Roj Women: Kurdish and Turkish Women's Rights, accessed June 3, 2011.
371. "About," Kurdish Women Against Honour Killing (KWAHK), accessed August 27, 2011.
372. Gorman and Mojab, "Dispersed Nationalism," p. 61.
373. "About." For more information about the Kurdish Women's Rights Watch (KWRW), see http://www.kwrw.org/, accessed August 27, 2011.
374. Yüksel, "The Encounter of Kurdish Women," p. 780.
375. Çaha, "The Kurdish Women's Movement," p. 435.

to raise awareness of Kurdish women's problems and to discuss the "woman question" from the perspective of women.

Deniz claims that it was necessary to create these platforms due to the fact that the Turkish and Kurdish Left were "willing to discuss the woman question but always postponed [dealing with] the problem until after the 'revolution.' But the revolution never comes and the revolutionist never gives up their privileges."[376] Thus, although unique from each other in presentation and content, each of these publications identified common foes to the advancement of Kurdish women in Turkey. Each addressed "the traditional values prevalent in Kurdish society responsible for women's oppression, subordination and suicides;" criticized Kurdish political parties and their practices that, initially, excluded women and women's views; and cited the debilitating effects of "victimizations experienced by Kurdish women (rape, torture, and migration) carried out by the state as deliberate policy."[377] For Deniz and her colleagues, these publications created a space for women to write and discuss the difficult issues of "discriminations, exclusions, domestic violence, and sexual abuse and so on," in the public sphere, which, at the time was "nearly closed to women" entirely.[378]

Notably, several of these journals were mostly published in Turkish. Deniz lists three reasons for this. First, although public use of Kurdish was legal by the time the magazines went to press, it was still dangerous to publish in Kurdish. Second, due to the decades-long moratorium on the use of Kurdish in both the public and private sphere, many urban Kurds did not and still do not know how to speak, write, or read in Kurdish.[379] Consequently, although the publishers of these journals encouraged submissions in Kurdish, not many contributors were able to write well enough in their mother tongue,[380] and editorial obstacles arose as well.[381] Third, by publishing in Turkish it was possible to continue the attempt to build bridges with Turkish women and to speak to Turkish audiences "about the Kurdish issue and the problems of Kurdish women, or the problems that women faced as being Kurdish."[382] Despite the challenges, overall, Fatma

376. Dilşa Deniz, founder, editorial board member, and contributor to *Jujin* and *Roza*, E-mail Interview, May 11, 2013.
377. Çaha, "The Kurdish Women's Movement," pp. 441–443.
378. Dilşa Deniz, E-mail Interview, May 11, 2013.
379. Ibid.
380. Çaha, "The Kurdish Women's Movement," p. 447, note 4.
381. Dilşa Deniz, E-mail Interview, May 11, 2013.
382. Ibid.

Kayhan, owner and editor of *Roza*, coined these years as the "Kurdish women's renaissance."[383]

To that effect, *Roza* and *Jujin*, which began publishing in 1996 and 1997, respectively, were explicitly created by Kurdish women who sought to differentiate their point of view from those of the Kurdish nationalist movement (PKK-led), Kurdish men, and the perspective of Turkish women as well.[384] Most of these women were college graduates and had left-leaning political backgrounds. According to Deniz, the women who launched *Roza* and *Jujin* had no engagement or affiliation with political parties or groups. Furthermore, these magazines represented the first time that Kurdish women openly identified as feminists and used "feminist ideology, language, and approach to deal with the Kurdish woman question."[385] After a few years of publication, Turkish women, Armenian women, and lesbians began contributing articles, too.[386]

In his article, "The Kurdish Women's Movement: A Third-Wave Feminism Within the Turkish Context," Ömer Çaha convincingly argues that through an examination of the Kurdish feminist publications that appeared in the mid-1990s, it is possible to see that although the Kurdish women's movement "evolved in the corridors of the leftist movements of the 1970s and ethnic movements of the 1980s,"[387] today there exists a unique, "Kurdish feminist identity constructed upon the meeting point of the dual oppressions" of being a Kurd and being female.[388] At first, proponents of the national movement did not accept this distinctively feminist movement. According to Deniz, the publications and the women behind them were challenged by Kurdish political groups who were shocked by the content and threatened by the possible splintering of the Kurdish political community they feared the magazines would cause. But, eventually, they were accepted. She also claims that there were those who said such topics were not newsworthy and certainly not fit for print media. Nevertheless, after the Kurdish weekly journal, *Azadiya Welat (Freedom of the Country)*, covered the story of the Kurdish feminist movement in a positive light, Kurdish political media showed interest and support in their work, and even allowed these women to use their offices and computers to design the magazines.[389]

---

383. Çaha, "The Kurdish Women's Movement," p. 435.
384. Yüksel, "The Encounter of Kurdish Women," p. 785.
385. Dilşa Deniz, E-mail Interview, May 11, 2013.
386. Ibid.
387. Çaha, "The Kurdish Women's Movement," p. 447.
388. Ibid., p. 446.
389. Dilşa Deniz, E-mail Interview, May 11, 2013.

Meeting the Challenges that Remain:
Tempering Progress with the Long Road Ahead

In addition to fighting for her freedom from Turkish authorities that sought to terminate her career, Leyla Zana had to overcome the impediments of sexism and conservatism within her own society as well. In *Writings from Prison* she recounted an early parliamentary group meeting in which one of her colleagues, "known as a democrat and a progressive," interrupted her, insisting that men should speak first, "as in our good old patriarchal tradition!" Shocked by his outburst, Leyla Zana patiently explained to her co-parliamentarian that she received twice the number of votes that he had in the election and that her job was to speak out for her constituency, wherever necessary, and that she had "as much right to speak as anyone else."[390] Wanting to be considered a human being and to express herself on an equal basis with men, Leyla Zana stated that while putting the concept of equality into practice was a lengthy process, the men of her party "finally got used to it."[391]

Kurdish women of Turkey continue to straddle a dichotomous existence between yesterday's expectations and the future's aspirations — for political and civil rights in Turkey, as well as gender rights within the Kurdish community itself. Today, many Kurdish women remain confined to the private sphere and are constricted by the social mores and structures established by a traditional, conservative, Muslim, patriarchal, and tribal society whose powerholders cling tenaciously to their grip on the present. This ongoing reality renders Kurdish women, as a group, possessions of their societies rather than full, independent human beings.

Yet, there is a clear indication that, in their struggle against and within the Turkish state, Kurdish women have begun to carve out a new destiny framed by their specific experience as Kurdish women in Turkey. From democratic political participation, to citizen-based women's rights initiatives, academic literary magazines, and employment outside of the home, presently Kurdish women in Turkey are well positioned to continue improving their plight. In contrast, thirty years ago, a Kurdish woman fighting for her rights as a woman and as a Kurd could only turn to the PKK to pursue these aspirations, and such involvement sometimes came at a very high price. Twenty-five years ago, few to none of these grassroots advocacy groups existed, and the number of Kurdish women who could lead them were negligible.

---

390. Zana, Writings from Prison, p. 1.
391. Ibid.

Today, Kurdish women have a choice in how to participate in their national movement and, in addition, now lead a parallel gender parity struggle. Although not yet equal to the demand, they have increasing access to resources that allow them to continue on a trajectory in which more Kurdish women can overcome historic obstacles to the embodiment of their full human potential, exercise choice and agency, and pursue the lifestyles they desire. Regardless of the final outcome of the Kurdish national struggle, the Kurdish women's rights movement will certainly carry on.

Sources Cited and Consulted

Archive Materials

Destani, B., ed. *Minorities in the Middle East: Kurdish Communities, 1918–1974*, Vol. 1, 1918–1930. Document 2, Despatch No. 1268/M1743 from Sir A. Calthorpe, High Commissioner, Constantinople, to Earl Curzon of Keddleston, Secretary of State for the Colonies, 23 July 1919, enclosing a paper titled "Notes on the Kurdish Situation," by Major E.W.C. Noel, Constantinople, 18 July 1919, together with paper titled "Mesopotamia: British Relations with Kurdistan" by the Political Department, India Office, 27 August 1919 [FO608/95]. Archive Editions Ltd., 2006, pp. 72–108.

Destani, B., ed. *Minorities in the Middle East: Kurdish Communities, 1918–1974*, Vol. 3, 1941–1967. Document 71, Confidential despatch [sic] No. 117 (1631/4/51) from Mr. D. Scott-Fox, British Embassy, Ankara, to Mr. H. Morrison, Foreign Office, 21 May 1951, enclosing a confidential report by Mr. Arthur, Second Secretary at Ankara Embassy, undated title "A tour in South East Anatolia during April 1951," [FO248/1523]. Archive Editions Ltd., 2006.

Books

Bengio, Ofra, ed. *Kurdish Awakening: Nation Building in a Fragmented Homeland*. Austin: University of Texas Press, 2014.

Edmonds, C.J. *Kurds, Turks and Arabs: Politics, Travel and Research in Northern Iraq, 1919–1925*. London: Oxford University Press, 1957.

Gross, Avraham. *Pious and Rebellious: Jewish Women in Medieval Europe*. Walthan, MASS: Brandeis Unversity Press, 2004.

Gunes, Cengiz. *The Kurdish National Movment: From Protest to Resistance*. New York: Routledge, 2012.

Hansen, H.H. *The Kurdish Woman's Life: Field Research in Muslim Society, Iraq*, Copenhagen: Nationalmuseets Skrifter, Etnografisk, Roekke VII, 1961.

Kaufman, Shirley, Galit Hasan-Rokem, and Tamar S. Hess. *The Defiant Muse: Hebrew Feminist Poems from Antiquity: A Bilingual Anthology*. The Helen Rose Scheuer Jewish Women's Series. New York: The Feminist Press at City University of New York, 1999.

Laizer, Sheri. *Into Kurdistan: Frontiers Under Fire*. London and New Jersey: Zed Books, 1991.

Lewis, Bernard. *The Emergence of Modern Turkey*. Second Edition. London: Oxford University Press, 1969.

Marcus, Aliza. *Blood and Belief: the PKK and the Kurdish Fight for Independence*. New York and London: New York University Press, 2007.

McKiernan, Kevin. *The Kurds: A People in Search of Their Homeland*. New York: St. Martin's Press, 2006.

Moghadam, Valentine M. *Gender and Nationality: Women and Politics in Muslim Societies*. London and New Jersey: Zed Books, Ltd., 1994.

Mojab, Shahrzad, ed. *Women Of A Non-State Nation: The Kurds*. Costa Mesa, CA: Mazda Publishers, 2001.

Özcan, Ali Kemal. *Turkey's Kurds: A Theoretical Analysis of the PKK and Abdullah Öcalan*. London and New York: Routledge, Taylor & Francis Group, 2006.

Papanek, Hanna. "The Ideal Woman and the Ideal Society: Control and Autonomy in the Construction of Identity." In: V.M. Moghadam (ed.), *Identity Politics and Women*. Boulder, CO: Westview Press, 1994.

Romano, David. *The Kurdish Nationalist Movement: Opportunity, Mobilization, and Identity*. Cambridge: Cambridge University Press, 2006.

Soane, E.B. *To Mesopotamia and Kurdistan in Disguise*, Second Edition. London: J. Murray, 1926.

Yapp, M.E. *The Making of the Modern Near East 1792–1923*. London and New York: Longman Group UK Limited, 1987.

Yuval-Davis, Nira. *Gender and Nation*. London: Sage Publications, 1997.

Zana, Leyla. *Writings from Prison*. Watertown, Massachussetts: Blue Crane Books, 1999.

Academic Journals

Ahamzadeh, Hashem. "The World of Kurdish Women's Novels." *Iranian Studies*, Vol. 41, No. 5 (December 2008), pp. 719–738.

Arat, Yeşim. "Democracy and Women in Turkey: In Defense of Liberalism." *Social Politics*, Vol. 6, No. 3 (Fall 1999), pp. 370–387. Oxford University Press.

van Bruinessen, Martin. "Turkey's Death Squads." *Middle East Report*, No. 99. Turkey: Insovlent Ideologies, Fractured State, (April–June 1996), Middle East Research and Information Project (MERIP), p. 20.

Çaha, Omer. "The Kurdish Women's Movement: A Third-Wave Feminism Within the Turkish Context." *Turkish Studies*, Vol. 12, No. 3 (September 2011), pp. 435–449.

Dönmez, Rasim Özgur. "Book Review: *Dağın Ardına Bakmak (Looking Beyond the Mountain)*." *Ethnopolitics*, Vol. 11, Issue 1 (March 2012), pp. 117–119.

Fuller, Graham E. "The Fate of the Kurds." *Foreign Affairs*, Vol. 72, No. 2 (Spring 1993), pp. 108–121.

Güzeldere, Ekrem Eddy. "Turkey: Regional Elections and the Kurdish Question." *Caucasian Review of International Affairs*, Volume 3, Number 3 (Summer 2009), pp. 291–306. http://cria-online.org/8_5.html. Accessed August 28, 2012.

Hassanpour, Amir. "The Kurdish Experience." *Middle East Report* No. 189, (July–August 1994), pp. 2–7.

Ilkkaracan, Pinar and Women for Women's Human Rights. "Exploring the Context of Women's Sexuality in Eastern Turkey." *Reproductive Health Matters*, Vol. 6, No. 12, Sexuality (November 1998), pp. 66–75.

İnce Hlal Onur, Aysun Yarali, and Doğancan Özsel. "Customary Killings in Turkey and Turkish Modernization." *Middle Eastern Studies*, Vol. 45, No. 4 (July 2009), pp. 537–551.

Karlsson, Helena. "Politics, Gender, and Genre — The Kurds and 'The West': *Writings from Prison* by Leyla Zana." *Journal of Women's History*, Vol. 15, No. 3 (Autumn 2003), pp. 158.

King, Diane E. "The Personal is Patrilineal: **Namus** as Sovereignty." *Identities: Global Studies in Culture and Power*, Vol. 15, No. 3 (2008), pp. 317–342.

Kutschera, Chris. "A Silent Scream." *The Middle East*. London. No. 27 (October 1993), pp. 33–35.

Mamikonian, Sargis. "Israel and the Kurds (1949–1990)." *Iran & the Caucusus*, Vol. 9, No. 2 (2005), pp. 381–399.

Mojab, Shahrzad. "Nationalism and Feminism: The Case of Kurdistan." In *Institute Simone de Beauvoir Bulletin*. Montreal: Concordial University Press (1995), pp. 65–73.

Mojab, Shahrzad, and Rachel Gorman. "Dispersed Nationalism: War, Diaspora and Kurdish Women's Organizing." *Journal of Middle East Women's Studies*, Vol. 3, No. 1 (Winter 2007), pp. 58–85.

Mojab, Shahrzad. "The Politics of 'Cyberfeminism' in the Middle East: The Case of Kurdish Women." *Race, Gender & Class*, Vol. 8, No. 4 (2001), pp. 42–61.

Nagengast, Carole. "Women, Minorities, and Indigenous Peoples: Universalism and Cultural Relativity." *Journal of Anthropological Research*, Vol. 53, No. 3, Universal Human Rights versus Cultural Relativity (Autumn 1997), pp. 349–369.

Öktem, Kerem. "Harbingers of Turkey's Second Republic." *Middle East Report* (August 1, 2007). Middle East Research and Information Project (MERIP). http://www.merip.org/mero/mero080107. Accessed May 22, 2011.

Özcan, Nihat Ali. "PKK Recruitment of Female Operatives." *Terrorism Focus*, Vol. 4, Issue 28, (September 11, 2007). http://www.jamestown.org/single/?no_cache=1&tx_ttnews[tt_news]=4394. Accessed August 27, 2011.

Secor, Anna. "'There is an Istanbul That Belongs to Me': Citizenship, Space and Identity in the City." *Annals of the Association of American Geographers*, Vol. 94, No. 2 (June 2004), pp. 352–368. Published by Taylor and Francis, Ltd., on behalf of the *Association of American Geographers*.

Sezgin, Ufuk and Raija-Leena Punamaki. "Effectiveness of Group Psychotherapy Among Women with Multiple Traumatic Life Events: A Pilot Study in the Southeast Anatolian Region." *Journal of Loss and Trauma*, Vol. 13, No. 6 (2008), pp. 557–575.

Sykes, Mark. "The Kurdish Tribes of the Ottoman Empire." *The Journal of the Royal Anthropological Institute of Great Britain and Ireland,* Vol. 38 (Jul.–Dec. 1908), pp. 451–486.

Watts, Nicole F. "Allies and Enemies: Pro-Kurdish Parties in Turkish Politics, 1990–1994." *International Journal of Middle East Studies,* Vol. 31, No. 4 (November 1999), pp. 631–656. Cambridge University Press.

White, J.B. "State Feminism, Modernization, and the Turkish Republican Woman." *NWSA Journal,* Vol. 15, No. 3, Gender and Modernism Between the Wars (2003), pp. 145–159.

Yüksel, Metin. "The Encounter of Kurdish Women with Nationalism in Turkey." *Middle Eastern Studies,* Vol. 42, No. 5 (September 2006), pp. 777–802. Routledge, Taylor & Francis Group.

Online and News Sources

"Abdullah Öcalan, A Short Biography." Partiya Karkerên Kurdistanê (PKK). http://www.pkkonline.com/en/index.php?sys=article&artID=22. Accessed on August 29, 2011.

"About." Kurdish Women Against Honour Killing (KWAHK). http://www.kwrw.org/kwahk/. Accessed August 27, 2011.

"About." Kurdish Women's Rights Watch (KWRW). http://www.kwrw.org/. Accessed August 27, 2011.

"About Us." *Roj Women: Kurdish and Turkish Women's Rights.* http://rojwomn.com/about/. Accessed June 3, 2011.

Akrayi, Aryan. "Asenath Barzani." *Kurdistan's Women Blog.* April 9, 2008. http://kurdistanwomen.blogspot.com/2008/04/asenath-barzani.html. Accessed January 29, 2012.

Albayrak, Ayla and JoeParkinson, "Turkey Reinstates Kurdish Candidates." *The Wall Street Journal,* April 22, 2011. http://online.wsj.com/article/SB10001424052748704071704576276912510860024.html. April 23, 2011.

Ali, Othman. "What Kurds will lose if AKP loses at the elections." *Today's Zaman*, June 9, 2011. http://www.sundayszaman.com/sunday/newsDetail_getNewsById.action?newsId=246755. Accessed August 28, 2012.

Al-Jazeera. "Kurdish Activist to Form New Party," *Al-Jazeera*, Archive, October 22, 2004. http://english.aljazeera.net/archive/2004/10/200849155826607676.html. Accessed July 10, 2011.

Akgül, Elif. "29 Ay Sonra Gelen Serbestliği Konşutular," *Bianet*, May 13, 2014, http://www.bianet.org/bianet/medya/155626-29-ay-sonra-gelen-serbestligi-konustular. Accessed January 7, 2015.

Alpay, Sahin. "Future of the Kurdish question in Turkey." *Today's Zaman*, January 1, 2012. http://www.todayszaman.com/columnist-267343-future-of-the-kurdish-question-in-turkey.html. Accessed February 1, 2012.

ANF News Agency. "Former DTK co-chair Yüksel Genç arrested." *ANF* News Agency. October 31, 2011. http://en.firatnews.com/index.php?rupel=article&nuceID=3424. Accessed February 5, 2012.

Anzia, Lys. "Suffering Without A Nation — The Plight of Kurdish Women in the Diaspora." *Women's News Network*. February 14, 2008. http://womensnewsnetwork.net/2008/02/14/suffering-without-a-nation-%E2%80%93-the-plight-of-kurdish-women-in-the-diaspora/. Accessed on December 22, 2011.

Argue, Steven. "Kurdish Culture, Repression, Women's Rights, and Resistance." June 12, 2007. http://www.indybay.org/newsitems/2007/06/12/18426957.php. Accessed on April 30, 2011.

"Asnat Barzani, Asenath Barzani 1590-1670 CE." *Womenphilosophers.com*. http://www.women-philosophers.com/Asnat-Barzani.html. Accessed January 22, 2012.

Aybars, Idil. "Seeking real equality for Turkey's women." *Common Ground News Service*, November 25, 2011. http://www.commongroundnews.org/print_article.php?artId=30699&... Accessed on November 25, 2011.

Bagikhani, Nazand. "Kurdish Women and National Identity." *KurdishMedia.com*. November 8, 2003. Accessed from http://kwahk.org/articles.asp?id=37, April 30, 2011.

BBC Turkey. "12 Haziran'da seçilen kadın milletvekilleri 'rekor' kırdı," (12 June the record of Elected Women MPs is Broken.) *BBC Turkey,* June 13, 2011. http:// www.bbc.co.uk/turkce/haberler/2011/06/110613_turkish_elections_women_ minorities.shtml. Accessed June 30, 2011.

Bernard, Eva. "Women and the Kurdish Movement in Turkey: 'There will be no turning back." *The WVoice,* Vol. 2, No. 4, May 8, 2014. http://womensvoicesnow. org/wvoice/women_and_the_kurdish_movement_in_turkey_there_will_be_ no_turning_back. Accessed May 24, 2014.

Bianet, "In 2016, Men Killed 261 Women." An infographic published by *Bianet* with the financial support of the Friedrich Ebert Stiftung and the Swedish International Development Cooperation Agency. The data reported are based on news reports from national, local, and Internet media in Turkey between January 1, 2016 and December 31, 2016.

Bilefsky, Dan. "Isiklar Journal: Polygamy Fosters Culture Clashes (and Regrets) in Turkey." *New York Times,* July 10, 2006.

Bozkurt, Goksel. "Turkish PM meets Kurdish MPs on immunity lifting row." *Hürriyet Daily News,* December 14, 2012. http://www.hurriyetdailynews. com/turkish-pm-meets-kurdish-mps-on-immunity-lifting-row. aspx?pageID=238&nid=36826. Accessed April 23, 2013.

Butler, Daren. "Turkish court convicts Turkish politician over speeches." *Reuters News Service,* May 24, 2012. www.euronews.com/newswires/1528072-turkish-court-convicts-kurdish-politician-over-speeches/. Accessed July 9, 2012.

Çağaptay, Soner. "Women 'appear' in Turkey's Parliament." *Hürriyet Daily News and Economic Review,* Sunday, July 17, 2011. http://www.hurriyetdailynews. com/n.php?n=women-8216appear8217-in-turkey8217s-parliament-2011-07-17. Accessed August 20, 2011.

Çağaptay, Soner. "'Kurdish Opening' Closed Shut." *Foreign Policy,* October 28, 2009. http://www.foreignpolicy.com/articles/2009/10/28/kurdish_opening_ closed_shut?page=0,1, Accessed August 28, 2012.

Committee to Protect Journalists. "Ocak Isik Yurtcu, Former editor in chief, Ozgur Gundem, Turkey, Currently Serving a 15-year Prison Sentence for Disseminating 'Separatist Propaganda'." *Committee to Protect Journalists.* https://cpj.org/awards96/yurtcu.html. Accessed August 3, 2012.

Daily Sabah. "Political ban of pro-Kurdish politicians ends as they seek to join HDP," *Daily Sabah*, Politics, Politics, December 17, 2014. http://www. dailysabah.com/politics/2014/12/17/political-ban-of-prokurdish-politicians-ends as-they-seek-to-join-hdp. Accessed January 28, 2015.

Damon, Arwa. "Female Fighters: We won't stand for male dominance." *Cnn. com International*, October 6, 2008. http://edition.cnn.com/2008/WORLD/ meast/10/06/iraq.pkk/. Accessed August 24, 2011.

Das, Bijoyeta. "For Better or Worse, Sister Swapping Persists." *Women's e-News*, March 22, 2010. http://www.womensenews.org/story/ marriagedivorcemotherhood/100319/better-or-worse-sister-swapping-persists?page=0,1. Accessed April 23, 2011.

"Demokratik Özgür Kadın Hareketi kuruldu," *SAVAS KARSITLARI*, September 18, 2003, http://www.savaskarsitlari.org/arsiv.asp?ArsivTipID=5&ArsivAna ID=15806, accessed April 25, 2013.

Doğan, Yonca Poyraz. "Turkish Women face discrimination, violence, illiteracy despite small gains." *Today's Zaman*, March 7, 2012. http://www.todayszaman. com/news-273620-.html. Accessed April 22, 2013.

Dugulin, Riccardo. "The Kurds' place in the 'Arab Spring'." *Open Democracy*, December 10, 2011. http://www.opendemocracy.net/riccardo-dugulin/kurds% E2%80%99-place-in-%E2%80%98arab-spring%E2%80%99. Accessed December 13, 2011.

EKurd.net, "Turkish court sentences Kurdish MP to jail for Kurdish PKK rebel remarks." *EKurd.net*, February 5, 2009. http://www.ekurd.net/mismas/ articles/misc2009/2/turkeykurdistan2097.htm. Accessed March 25, 2011.

Genç, Yüksel. "Who is deceiving whom?" *ANF News Agency*, January 23, 2012. http://en.firatnews.com/index.php?rupel=article&nuceID=3962. Accessed on February 5, 2012.

Gusten, Suzanne. "Sensing a Siege, Kurds Hits Back in Turkey." *New York Times*, March 21, 2012. http://www.nytimes.come/2012/03/21/world/europe/ sensing-a-siege-... Accessed March 22, 2012.

Haynes, Deborah "The Kurdish women rebels who are ready to fight and die for the Kurdish cause." *KurdNet*. October 24, 2007. http://www.ekurd.net/

mismas/articles/misc2007/10/turkeykurdistan1455.htm Accessed August 28, 2011.

Hürriyet Daily News. "Kurdish women fight for rights of both groups, Istanbul deputy says." *Hürriyet Daily News,* June 30, 2010. www.hurriyetdailynews. com/n.php?n=kurdish-women-fight-for-woman-rights-deputy-says-2010-06-30.

Hürriyet Daily News. "DTP also to blame in Kurdish problem, says deputy." *Hürriyet Daily News.* July 29, 2009. http://www.hurriyetdailynews.com/ default.aspx?pageid=438&n=dtp-also-to-blame-in-kurdish-problem-says-deputy-2009-07-29. Accessed on February 5, 2012.

Hürriyet Daily News. "First academic research on PKK's demographics." *Hürriyet Daily News,* July 18, 2011.http://www.hurriyetdailynews.com/ default.aspx?pageid=438&n=first-academic-study-on-pkk-reveals-grassroots-of-terrorism-2011-07-18. Accessed on August 2, 2011.

Hürriyet Daily News. "Turkish PM Erdoğan, Zana to meet to discuss Kurdish issue." *Hürriyet Daily News,* June 30, 2012. www.hurriyetdailynews.com/ PrintNews.aspx?PageID=383&NID=24432. Accessed July 8, 2012.

Hürriyet Daily News. "Zana reveals details of Erdoğan meeting." *Hürriyet Daily News,* July 12, 2012. www.hurriyetdailynews.com/PrintNews. aspx?PageID=383&NID=25299. Accessed July 15, 2012.

Hürriyet Daily News "Kurds Should not lay down arms, deputy says." *Hürriyet Daily News,* January 10, 2012. http://www.huriyyetdailynews.com/PrintNews. aspx?PageID=383&. Accesed January 10, 2012.

Ilkkaracan, Pinar. "The 'Turkish Model': for whom?" *Open Democracy,* November 9, 2011. http://www.opendemocracy.net/5050/pinar-ilkkaracan/ turkish-model-for-whom. Accessed January 4, 2012.

Jones, Dorian. "Turkey: Kurds Boycott Mosques for Language Rights." *Eurasianet.org,* June 7, 2011. http://www.eurasianet.org/node/63639. Accessed August 28, 2012.

Kalnoky, Boris. "Feminists and terrorists? Women and the PKK." *Women in Focus,* April 14, 2010. http://www.sofeminine.co.uk/key-debates/women-and-the-pkk-d12319.html. Accessed, August 28, 2011.

KA-MER Foundation official website. www.kamer.org.tr. Accessed August 2, 2012.

Kandiyoti, Deniz. "A tangled web: the politics of gender in Turkey." *Open Democracy*, January 5, 2011. http://www.opendemocracy.net/5050/deniz-kandiyoti/tangled-web-politics-of-gender-in-turkey. Accessed January 13, 2011.

Kapuci, Selçuk. "PKK members: Ergenekon prevented our release." *Today's Zaman*. October 21, 2009. http://www.todayszaman.com/news-190569-pkk-members-ergenekon-prevented-our-release.html. Accessed February 5, 2012.

Karaman, Semanur. "Turkey elections mark the start of a revolution for women." *The Guardian*, June 19, 2015. http://www.theguardian.com/global-development/2015/jun/19/turkey-elections-revolution-hdp-women-female-mps. Accessed October 12, 2015.

Kışanak, Gültan, Nadje Al-Ali, and Latif Tas. "Kurdish women's battle continues against state and patriarchy, says first female co-mayor of Diyarbakir. Interview." *Open Democracy*. August 12, 2016. https://www.opendemocracy.net/nadje-al-ali-latif-tas-g-ltan-ki-anak/kurdish-women-s-battle-continues-against-state-and-patriarchy-. Accessed on August 14, 2016.

Koma Jinên Bilind. "The Kurdistan Women's Liberation Movement for a Universal Women's Struggle." The High Women's Council — KJB (Koma Jinên Bilind). March 2011. http://www.kjb-online.org/hakkimizda/?lang=en. Accessed May 26, 2014.

Kurd Net. "Kurdish Asenath Barzani, The first Jewish woman in history to become a Rubbi [sic]." *Kurd Net*, September 13, 2010. http://ekurd.net/mismas/articles/misc2010/9/state4196.htm. Accessed January 23, 2012.

Kurd Net. "Former prominent Kurdish legislator Leyla Zana hoping to make comeback in Turkey's June elections." *Kurd Net*, April 11, 2011. http://www.ekurd.net/mismas/articles/misc2011/4/turkey3181.htm. Accessed April 11, 2011.

Kurdistan Tribune. "Turkish court sentences Kurdish deputy Aysel Tugluk to two years' jail." *Kurdistan Tribune*, August 2, 2011. http://kurdistantribune.com/2011/turkish-court-sentences-aysel-tugluk-two-years-jail/. Accessed August 28, 2011.

"KURDISTAN: Kurdish Women in Southeast Turkey Grow Strong Support Networks." Originally printed in *Hürriyet Daily News*. December 10, 2010. Accessed from Peacewomen.org: http://www.peacewomen.org/news_article. php?id=2589&type=news. Accessed April 22, 2011.

Lyons, Cameron. "Why the EU Needs Turkey: A Case for Accession." *Northeastern University Political Review* (February 3, 2011). http://www. nupoliticalreview.com/?p=319, accessed June 26, 2013.

Melammed, Renee Levine. "Asnat Barazani." *Jewish Women's Archive, Jewish Women: A Comprehensive Historical Encyclopedia*. http://jwa.org/encyclopedia/article/barazani-asnat-bat-samuel. Accessed January 16, 2012.

Mohammed, Najeeba. "Iraqi brides pay high price." *ISN ETH Zurich*. March 20, 2007. http://www.isn.ethz.ch/isn/Digital-Library/Articles/Detail//?ots591=4888caa0-b3db-1461-98b9-e20e7b9c13d4&lng=en&id=53050. Accessed April 18, 2013.

Mojab, Shahrzad and Amir Hassanpour. "In Memory of Fadime Sahindal, Thoughts on the Struggle Against 'Honor Killing'." *KWAHK*, http://www. kwahk.org/articles.asp?id=30, October 17, 2002. Accessed on December 12, 2011.

Nielsen, Nikolaj. "Honor Killings and Turkey." *Human Rights: The World Affairs Blog Network, Foreign Policy Blogs*, March 28, 2009. http://humanrights. foreignpolicyblogs.com/2009/03/28/honor-killings-and-turkey/. Accessed April 25, 2011. Nurhak, Delal Afsin. "The Kurdistan Woman's Liberation Movement." Partiya Karkerên Kurdistan (PKK), http://www.pkkonline.com/en/index.php?sys=article&artID=180. Accessed May 24, 2014.

Nzibari. "The Iraqi Kurdish Prinicipalities." *Kurdish Musings — No Friends but the Mountains*. March 15, 2012. http://lepzerin.wordpress. com//?s=Khanzad&search=Go. Accessed May 8, 2013.

Öztürk, Merve Büşra. "Demands of Kurds and Zana." *Today's Zaman*. December 29, 2011. http://www.todayszaman.com/columnist-267110-demands-of-kurds-and-zana.html. Accessed January 2, 2012.

"Patriarchy — the Enslavement of Women." From: "All Articles" on the Partiya Karkerên Kurdistanê (PKK) website, in English. http://www.pkkonline.com/en/index.php?sys=article&artID=56. Accessed August 21, 2011.

Pizzi, Michael. "Kurdish election gains are 'historic' boost for inclusion in Turkey." *Al-Jazeera America*, June 9, 2015. http://america.aljazeera.com/articles/2015/6/9/kurdish-gains-in-parliament-mark-historic-turn-for-turkish-pluralism.html. Accessed October 12, 2015.

Porter, Kathryn Cameron. "Disappearances — an Alarming Trend." *American Kurdish Information Network* (AKIN), January 2, 1997. http://kurdistan.org/work/commentary/disappearances-an-alarming-trend/. Accessed August 22, 2012.

Radikal. "Yine Vekil " ("Representative Wants More"). *Radikal*, October 1, 2011. http://www.radikal.com.tr/Radikal.aspx?aType=RadikalDetayV3&ArticleID=1065034&Date=01.10.2011&CategoryID=78. Accessed October 2, 2011.

Rigoni, Isabelle. "Conclusion of the conference 'Women, violence and the politics of mobilizing resistance: the case of Kurdish women." KWAHK. February 22, 2002. http://www.kwahk.org/articles.asp?id=31. Accessed December 29, 2011.

Rojwomen.com. "Leyla Zana: No freedom without women's freedom." *Rojwomen.com*, March 12, 2011. http://rojwomen.com/2011/03/12/zana-no-freedom-without-womens-freedom/. Accessed April 30, 2011.

Rojwomen.com. "72 Women killed in the past year in South East Turkey." *Rojwomen.com*, March 12, 2011. Translated by Berna Özgencil. http://rojwomen.com/2011/03/12/72-women-killed-in-the-past-year-in-the-south-east/. Accessed April 22, 2011.

S, Eda. "We Can Change…" Finalist in WLPS Youth Essay Contest Group 2: 18–25 years. January 16, 2011. http://wwwlearningpartnership.org/blog/2010/turkey-kurdish-women/. Accessed April 25, 2011.

Schemm, Paul. "Kurdish fighters offer guerilla feminism." *AFP*, November 28, 2006. Found on: *Kurdish Aspect — Kurdish News and Points of View*. http://www.kurdishaspect.com/Kurdishfightersofferguerrillafeminism.html. Accessed August 28, 2011.

Schleifer, Yigal. "Dreams of Kurdistan." *Foreign Policy*, May 25, 2012. http://www.foreignpolicy.com/articles/2012/05/25/dreams_of_kurdistan?page=0,1. Accessed August 28, 2012.

Sehlikoğlu, Sertaç. "Rape in Turkey: between incitement, complicity and silence." *Open Democracy*, March 18, 2011, https://www.opendemocracy. net/5050/serta%C3%A7-sehliko%C4%9Flu/rape-in-turkey-between-incitement-complicity-and-silence, Accessed March 21, 2011.

Sert, Aysegul. "A Woman, A Kurd, and An Optimist." *The New York Times: The Female Factor*. February 19, 2013. http://www.nytimes.com/2013/02/20/world/europe/20iht-letter20.html?_r=2&. Accessed February 22, 2013.

Stewart, Catrina. "Combined Revolutions Begin to Bear Fruit for Kurdish Women Guerillas." *The Irish Times*. November 11, 2010. http://www.irishtimes. com/newspaper/world/2010/1113/1224283235214.html. Accessed January 8, 2012.

Sugden, Jonathan and Sunar Yurdatapan. "Kurdish Political Leader Leyla Zana Released After Decade in Jail." *Democracy Now!*, June 4, 2010. http:// www.democracynow.org/2004/6/10/kurdish_political_prisoner_leyla_zana_ released. Accessed April 18, 2013.

Sussman, Anna Louie. "Why Turkey is Backsliding on Women's Rights." *The Atlantic*, June 16, 2011. http://www.theatlantic.com/international/archive/2011/06/why-turkey-is-backsliding-on-womens-rights/240547. Accessed June 27, 2011.

Tamet, Meral. "Can Erdogan Make Room for Women in the AKP Congress." *Al-Monitor*, September 28, 2012.http://www.al-monitor.com/pulse/politics/2012/09/female-political-representation-in-turkey-room-for-improvement. html. Accessed April 22, 2013. Original article: "Can Prime Minister Open up Space for Women in AKP Congress?" Published by *Milliyet* (Turkish). Translated by Timur Goksel.

The Kurdish Globe. "BDP's second congress: Is the destination Ankara or is it Kurdistan?" *The Kurdish Globe*, September 10, 2011. http://www.kurdishglobe. net/display-article.html?id=C301773E51DFD77C897D64EF6781803C. Accessed October 1, 2011.

Today's Zaman. "Pro-Kurdish deputy Zana says weapons 'insurance of Kurds'." *Today's Zaman*. January 10, 2012. http://www.todayszaman.com/news-268145-pro-kurdish-deputy-zana-says-weapons-insurance-of-kurds.html. Accessed January 10, 2012.

Today's Zaman. "Future of the Kurdish question in Turkey." *Today's Zaman*. January 1, 2012.http://www.todayszaman.com/columnist-267343-future-of-the-kurdish-question-in-turkey.html. Accessed January 2, 2012.

Today's Zaman. "PKK Ceasefire end seen as move to help BDP before elections." *Today's Zaman*, March 2, 2011. http://www.todayszaman.com/newsDetail_getNewsById.action?newsId=237075. Accessed March 1, 2012.

Today's Zaman. "Kurdish deputy sentenced to 14.5 years in prison." *Today's Zaman*, June 12, 2012. http://www.todayszaman.com/newsDetail_getNewsById.action?newsId=283289. Accessed August 29, 2012.

Today's Zaman. "PKK members: Ergenekon prevented our release," *Today's Zaman*, October 21, 2010. http://www.sundayszaman.com/sunday/newsDetail_getNewsById.action?newsId=190569. Accessed February 2, 2012.

Utell, Janine. "The Woman Question," *The Modernist Journals Project*. A joint project of Brown University and University of Tulsa. http://www.modjourn.org/render.php?view=mjp_object&id=mjp.2005.00.088. Accessed March 14, 2015.

van Wilgenburg, Wladimir. "PKK and Islamic Gulen Movement Clash in Turkey." *Rudaw.net*, December 18, 2010. http://www.rudaw.net/english/science/op-ed-contributors/3370.html. Accessed November 5, 2012.

Yavuz, Ercan. "Tuğluk case risks turning into another Zana scandal." *Today's Zaman*, February 9, 2009. http://www.todayszaman.com/newsDetail_getNewsById.action;jsessionid=16C7C9784DFA6C35E717580D0DAFE9ED?load=detay&link=166402&bolum=101&newsId=166330. Accessed February 5, 2012.

Non-Governmental Organization and Governmental Organization Reports and Documents

Amnesty International. "TURKEY: The colours of their clothes: parliamentary deputies serve 15 years' imprisonment for expressions of Kurdish political identity." Amnesty International, December 1997. AI Index: EUR44/85/97.

Amnesty International. "Turkey: End sexual violence against women in custody!" Amnesty International, February 26, 2003. AI Index: EUR 44/006/2003.

Amnesty International. "VICTORY: Leyla Zana — Special Focus Case." Amnesty International, June 9, 2004. http://www.amnestyusa.org/our-work/latest-victories/leyla-zana-special-focus-case. Accessed on May 22, 2012.

Baser, Bahar. "Kurdish Diaspora Political Activism in Europe with a Particular Focus on Great Britain." Berghof Peace Support and Centre for Just Peace and Democracy, 2011.

Campbell Brenda and Michael Ivers. "Indiscriminate Use of Force: Violence in South-east Turkey Fact-Finding Mission Report." *KHRP and Bar Human Rights of Committee of England and Wales*, October 2006.

DÖKH (Demokratik Özgür Kadın Hareketi). "Call for Participation DÖKH's 1st Middle East Women's Conference Amed (Diyarbakır), Turkey, 31 May–2 June 2013." Association for Women's Rights in Development (AWID), March 13, 2013. http://www.awid.org/Library/Call-for-Participation-DOeKH-s-1st-Middle-East-Women-s-Conference-Amed-Diyarbakir-Turkey-31-May-2-June-2013. Accessed April 12, 2013.

European Federation of Journalists. "Latest News in Set Journalists Free in Turkey Campaign — Archive." European Federation of Journalists, March 10, 2013. http://europe.ifj.org/en/pages/latest-news-set-journalists-free-in-turkey-campaign-archive. Accessed March 10, 2013.

European Training Foundation (ETF). "Adult Literacy Education: Mothers and Daughters at School in Turkey." Prepared for the ETF by Hasan Terzi, Şeyda Kocacik, and Ayşe Ümit Öztekin. March 2011. http://www.etf.europa.eu/webatt.nsf/0/F0848DABBB254B06C125794A0035C5CB/$file/Adult%20literacy%20education_Turkey.pdf. Accessed February 1, 2012.

Human Rights Watch. "He Loves You, He Beats You: Family Violence in Turkey and Access to Protection." Human Rights Watch. May 4, 2011. http://www.hrw.org/en/reports/2011/05/04/he-loves-you-he-beats-you... Accessed May 26, 2011.

Human Rights Watch. *World Report 2012: Events of 2011*. Human Rights Watch, 2012. http://www.hrw.org/news/2012/01/22/world-report-2012-strengthen-support-arab-spring. Accessed January 25, 2012.

Human Rights Watch. "Time for Justice: Ending Impunity for Killings and Disappearances in 1990s Turkey." Human Rights Watch, September 2012.

http://www.hrw.org/sites/default/files/reports/turkey0912ForUpload.pdf. Accessed September 3, 2012.

Institut Kurde de Paris. "Information and liaison bulletin, No. 315, June 2011." Institute Kurde de Paris, June 2011, p. 3. http://www.institutkurde.org/en/publications/bulletins/pdf/315.pdf. Accessed December 23, 2011.

International Free Women's Foundation (Rotterdam, Utrecht University, Department of Clinical and Health Psychology) and Kurdistan Information Office, Paris, conducted and edited. "Psychological Consequences of Trauma Experiences on the Development of Migrated Kurdish Women in the European Union: Final Results and Background of a Survey in Five European Countries and Turkey." International Free Women's Foundation, Rotterdam, 2007.

KA-MER Foundation. "'Who's to Blame?" KA-MER "Project for the Development of Permanent Methods in the Struggle Against Killings Committed Under the Guise of 'Honor' in the Southeast and East Anatolia Regions, 2005 Report. The KA-MER Foundation, translated by Amy Spangler, 2005. www.wunrn.com/news/2006/05_08.../051306_turkey_kamer.doc. Accessed, December 29, 2011.

Kurdish Human Rights Project (KHRP). "The Increase in Kurdish Women Committing Suicide." European Parliament Project, Final Report. June 2007. Requested by the European Parliament's committee on Women Rights and Gender Equality. www.rojwomen.files.wordpress.com/2010/05/suicides-report.pdf. Accessed December 29, 2011.

Kurdish Human Rights Project (KHRP). "Trial Observation Report, Turkey's Shame: Sexual Violence Without Redress — The Plight of Kurdish Women." Kurdish Human Rights Project, December 2003.

Şancar, Serpil. "Final Report: Turkey: Country Gender Profile." Author is the director of the Women's Studies Center, Ankara University. AYÇA BULUT. December 2006. http://www.jica.go.jp/english/operations/thematic_issues/gender/background/pdf/e06tur.pdf. Accessed January 31, 2012.

"The Treaty of Sèvres, 1920, Section III, Articles 62–64." *The Treaties of Peace 1919–1923, Vol. 2*. New York: The Carnegie Endowment for Peace, 1924. http://wwi.lib.byu.edu/index.php/Section_I,_Articles_1_-_260. Accessed October 1, 2011.

"The Revolution in Kurdistan, 5th Congress, Kurdistan Workers Party (PKK), 24 January 1995: PKK Party Program, Chapter Three." Translated by Arm the Spirit. For A Free And Independent Kurdistan! KURD-L Archives — http://burn.ucsd.edu/archives/kurd-1. Accessed January 22, 2011.

Interviews and Conferences

Anonymous, Personal Interview. March 20, 2011.

Anonymous (same), E-mail Interview. September 28, 2012.

"Aysel Tuğluk." *Dersim 1938: 70 Years After*. A conference hosted by Feleknas Unca and sponsored by the European United Left/Nordic Green Left Parliamentary Group and the European Parliament. November 13, 2008, 3pm–6:30pm, EP, ASP 1G3. http://kurdistannytt.files.wordpress.com/2011/03/dersimconf1.pdf. Accessed January 12, 2012.

Baker, Awat (Liaison Officer to International Organizations, Department of Foreign Relations, Kurdistan Regional Government of Iraq), E-mail Interview. May 7, 2013.

Başol, Dünya. "The Impact of Religion on Kurdish Nationalism." Delivered to the *Forum on Kurdish Society, History and Culture* of the Moshe Dayan Center for Middle Eastern and African Studies, Tel Aviv University. Tel Aviv, Israel. April 2, 2012.

Deniz, Dilşa (founder, editorial board member, and contributor to *Jujin* and *Roza*), E-mail Interview. May 11, 2013.

Dryaz, Massoud Sharifi. "Women and nationalism: How women activists are changing the Kurdish conflict." Paper presented at conference at School Oriental Studies (SOAS), May 7–8, 2011. http://www.soas.ac.uk/lmei/events/ssemme/. Author provided URL and granted permission to cite via e-mail, August 21, 2012.

Sagnic, Ceng, Personal Interview. February 20, 2012.

Unal, Helin, E-mail Interviews. September 2, 2012, and September 7, 2012.

Zana, Leyla. "The role of Kurdish women in dialogue, conflict resolution, and reconstruction for democracy and peace." Statement given at Seminar hosted by Organization of Women's Freedom in Iraq (OWFI). May 24, 2008. Garden Court Chambers, 57–60 Lincoln's Inn Fields, WC2. http://www.equalityiniraq. com/activities/87-the-role-of-kurdish-women-in-dialogue-conflict-resolution-and-reconstruction-and-in-the-struggle-for-democracy-and-peace?6dcb5c0485-db6830947a0e9cf1d291b1=1...aa3c50e4d54095602988d54be. Accessed September 12, 2011.

Films and Documentaries

Al-Jazeera, "Witness — Turkey's Hidden Shame: Parts 1 & 2." Hosted on *Youtube.com*. February 10, 2009. https://www.youtube.com/watch?v=mdPzS-dI8WM.

Briand, Erwann (Director). *The Women of Mount Ararat*. A documentary film produced by Flight Movie Productions, 2004.

Das, Bijoyeta. *Saturday Mothers of Turkey* (short documentary, 2010). Hosted on the site of Women's Voices Now. http://womensvoicesnow.org/watchfilm/saturday_mothers_of_turkey1/.

Gol, Jiyar. "Turkey-Kurdish Woman, Leyla Zana," Short Documentary. Jiyar Films, 2006. http://www.youtube.com/watch?v=_ELe0MqNWGk.